THE ART OF STORYTELLING FOR FINANCIAL ADVISERS

Explaining Money Like a Human — Transforming Jargon into Stories Clients Never Forget

Mike LeGassick

COPYRIGHT © 2025 MIKE LEGASSICK

All rights reserved.

No part of this book may be reproduced, stored in a retrieval system, or transmitted in any form or by any means, electronic, mechanical, photocopying, recording, or otherwise, without the prior written permission of the publisher, except for brief quotations embodied in critical articles and reviews.

FOREWORD

I first met a financial adviser in 1978. I was a broker rep/inspector for National Employers Life (NEL) and my first ever meeting was at his home in Croydon. My job was the usual 'sell our products please' approach which took all of twenty minutes. We then went for a two-hour lunch.

The adviser concerned, Geoff - was in fact a Hambro Life salesman and not surprisingly his training had been very thorough. In particular his personal and soft skills. He was clearly very successful and had a beautiful home in the most prosperous part of town. What he told me over lunch I have never forgotten.

He complimented me on my positioning of NEL's income protection products but showed me how I might have had even more impact and that I might want to try this approach in future. As a brand-new broker rep straight out of the wrapper I was all ears.

He said that a great skill I should learn was telling stories – ideally drawing what I was saying on a note pad right in front of my prospect (in my case, financial advisers). He said that stories in a sales or marketing pitch always had far more impact – with the hand drawn element being the icing on the cake engaging more of the listener's senses. Even better if I could draw the accompanying image upside down so that the listener/viewer could see it their way round. He also showed me a neat trick with the pen which was used to guide the prospect's line of sight down from the paper and back up to make eye contact.

Forty-seven years later I still apply this learning as often as I can. When I run seminar and public speaking training for financial planners, telling stories is at the heart of getting your message across with clarity, confidence, authority, and conviction.

Over the years, the financial advice profession has gradually shifted its emphasis towards the technical aspects of the role, often at the expense of vital soft skills that help convey the true value of advice. Yet in my experience, it's these human, interpersonal skills – the ability to tell a story, paint a picture and bring clarity to complexity – that make all the difference. That's why I'm so delighted to see Mike championing this cause. His work is timely, and I'm confident that advisers, planners and IFAs across the profession will gain enormous value from his insights – and in turn, their clients will benefit too.

This book marks an important return to what really connects people – the power of storytelling. In an age when financial advice must be both technically sound and deeply human, Mike's book is not just a reminder of what we've been missing – it's a practical and inspiring guide to getting it back.

Philip Calvert – Financial Adviser Marketing Consultant

DEDICATION

---◇---

To all those who've shaped my journey in this profession—mentors, colleagues, and friends too numerous to name but whose generous wisdom and guidance have made me who I am today.

To my parents, no longer with me but forever present in everything I achieve, thank you for your unwavering support and boundless love.

And to Mary, my wife, whose love, understanding, and patience have been my constant foundation—thank you for always being there and having my back through every challenge and triumph.

This book exists because you all believed in me.

What Leading Voices in the Profession Are Saying About *The Art of Storytelling for Financial Advisers*

Storytelling is a hugely undervalued skill in financial planning. Done well, it makes abstract financial ideas relevant and memorable and fosters trust and understanding between the planner and the client.

Mike LeGassick is a master storyteller. Following the advice in this book will help you build a more profitable business and substantially increase the value you offer to clients.

— **Robin Powell, Journalist, Author, and Content Marketing Consultant to Advice Firms**

In a world of spreadsheets and stock tips, stories still win. The Art of Storytelling for Financial Advisers reveals the single most underrated skill in modern financial planning: the ability to connect through story.

Clients aren't craving charts or complex forecasts. They want meaning. They want clarity. They want to hear how their lives can be changed for the better through the advice you offer.

In an age dominated by AI and automation, it's not the most analytical that stand out—it's those who can make the complex feel simple, and the numbers feel personal.

This book is a timely and essential guide for any adviser who wants to win trust, inspire action, and build lasting relationships—one story at a time.

— **Alan Smith, Founder of Capital Partners; Host – Bulletproof Entrepreneur Podcast; Co-Host – The Rea Adviser Podcast**

The world of finance is noisy — and clients crave clarity. Mike's book is a quiet revolution, showing advisers how to use storytelling not just to explain, but to connect. It's a behavioural guide disguised as a storytelling manual — and every great adviser needs both.

Through practical frameworks and real-world examples, Mike demonstrates how narrative can transform complex financial concepts into compelling stories that clients understand, remember, and act upon.

In a profession drowning in jargon and data, this book is essential reading for advisers who want to break through the noise and create meaningful client relationships built on understanding.

— **Andy Hart, Founder of Humans Under Management & Behavioural Finance Advocate**

It has become fashionable in recent years to bring Behavioural Finance into conversations about advice, but there are a handful of people who have been highlighting this issue for over a decade. Mike is one of the originals and always worth listening to.

— **Ian McKenna, Founder & CEO AdviserSoftware.com**

CONTENTS

FOREWORD iii
DEDICATION v
ACKNOWLEDGEMENTS ix
INTRODUCTION xi
CHAPTER 1: The Noble Art of Empowering Clients 1
CHAPTER 2: Understanding the Power of Stories 39
CHAPTER 3: Crafting Compelling Narratives 51
CHAPTER 4: Creating Relatable Characters 65
CHAPTER 5: Setting the Scene: Context is King 77
CHAPTER 6: Simplifying Complex Concepts with Stories 129
CHAPTER 7: Building Trust Through Authentic Storytelling 165
CHAPTER 8: Engaging Your Audience 185
CHAPTER 9: Storytelling Across Different Media 193
CHAPTER 10: Case Studies and Practical Examples 203
CHAPTER 11: Ethics and Responsibility in Storytelling 209
CHAPTER 12: Practical Exercises for Financial Advisers 227
CHAPTER 13: Observing the Impact of Storytelling 241
CHAPTER 14: Conclusion 259
INDEX 268

ACKNOWLEDGEMENTS

---◇---

I would like to extend my sincere gratitude to Andy Hart of Humans Under Management and The Real Adviser Podcast (TRAP) for his invaluable insights and inspiration. His brilliant use of analogies has significantly shaped the way I communicate financial concepts, and I am grateful for the three inspirational analogies of his that I have included in this book: the rollercoaster, the swan ice sculpture, and the turkey at Christmas. His work, alongside his contributions to TRAP, continues to inspire financial advisers to engage clients in more meaningful and effective ways.

I want to recognise The Real Adviser Podcast (TRAP) and its presenters Alan Smith, Andy Hart, Carl Widger, and Nick Lincoln, who have been a valuable resource in shaping my thinking. Their insightful discussions on financial planning, behavioural finance, and industry trends have provided a wealth of knowledge and perspectives that have influenced many of the themes explored in this book. The podcast serves as an excellent platform for financial advisers seeking to refine their approach and stay ahead in an ever-evolving profession.

I would also like to acknowledge Robin Powell for his dedication as a thought leader in our profession. His relentless advocacy for transparency and evidence-based investing has had a profound impact on financial advisers and investors alike. His work has been instrumental in challenging outdated industry norms and promoting the principles of fairness, integrity, and long-term thinking. His influence was one of the key inspirations for writing this book, reinforcing my commitment to helping clients navigate their financial journey with clarity and confidence.

A special thank you to my friend, Philip Calvert, for writing the foreword to this book. Philip is a renowned global speaker whose expertise in marketing for IFAs has been invaluable. His insights into branding, communication, and client engagement have profoundly influenced how financial advisers present themselves and build trust in an increasingly digital world. His passion for elevating our profession is truly inspiring, and I deeply appreciate his generous contributions.

INTRODUCTION

Explaining Money Like a Human —
Transforming Jargon into Stories Clients Never Forget

Imagine navigating the complex world of financial advice with clarity, transforming technical discussions into meaningful conversations that genuinely connect with your clients. This book is your guide to moving beyond intimidating jargon toward understanding and trust.

Welcome to the art of financial storytelling—a powerful approach where narrative transforms client relationships. Whether you're newly qualified or an experienced adviser, this guide equips you with practical tools to excel beyond the numbers and create truly transformative connections with those you serve.

Our individual approaches as advisers can sometimes limit our communication. We become experts in products, calculations, and regulations—but remember, our technical expertise is just one element in the vast landscape of client experience. While professional knowledge forms the foundation of our service, it's essential to see the bigger picture: clients make decisions based on stories they can see themselves in, not spreadsheets they can barely decipher. True advisory wisdom comes from acknowledging this reality and seeing beyond the confines of financial terminology.

From ancient merchants sharing tales of trade routes to today's most successful advisers crafting compelling narratives about financial security, our inherent desire has always been to connect through story. This isn't just about explaining concepts; it's a journey towards creating understanding, trust, and a vision of a secure tomorrow that resonates on a human level.

The power of narrative, highlighted in studies across behavioural economics and psychology, is the cornerstone of exceptional financial advice. Consider the famous "elevator pitch" concept—in those brief moments, it's never the technical details that persuade, but the story that creates meaning. Similarly, your ability to transform complex financial strategies into compelling narratives isn't about simplifying information; it's about fulfilling your clients' psychological need for clarity and purpose.

For most clients, financial planning transcends the mere accumulation of wealth. It's the peace stemming from knowing their future is secure. Amidst the jargon and intricacies of financial markets, their predominant concern is not understanding every technical detail—it's the fear of making mistakes, missing opportunities, or running out of money. Beyond the complexities, people merely seek assurance for their and their families' futures, told in language that resonates with their lived experience.

By understanding the motivations that drive your clients and sidestepping the common communication pitfalls, you don't just aim for technical accuracy but align your advice with your clients' core desires and fears.

This book dispels myths clouding effective client communication and introduces core storytelling concepts like emotion, metaphor, timing, and relatable characters. You'll learn about human behaviour's impact on financial choices and how to craft narratives that align with long-term goals while addressing immediate concerns. You'll discover how different generations—from Baby Boomers to Generation Z—respond to stories through their unique cultural and experiential lenses, and how to adapt your narrative approach accordingly.

While foundational principles are discussed, remember that storytelling, like financial advice itself, is deeply personal. It requires adapting strategies to individual clients, their unique circumstances, and their personal goals. Developing your storytelling ability is also a lifelong learning process. Armed with the strategies and insights from this book, you'll stay grounded amidst the industry's push for more products and solutions, focusing instead on the human connection that truly drives client decisions.

Throughout, I share insights from my own journey working with financial advisers and their transformations through storytelling. But while this guide provides a comprehensive approach, it isn't a universal script. Your relationship with each client is unique. The stories you craft must reflect both your authentic voice and your client's individual narrative.

When clients walk into your office, they often can't wait to discuss their pension options, ISAs, or money they've inherited. That's completely natural. They've brought their statements, rehearsed their questions, and feel a responsibility to lay everything on the table. But in these moments, your job isn't to jump straight into the numbers — it's to help them take a breath, slow things down, and gently take control of the meeting.

Guide the conversation back to the person, not the paperwork. Before you give any answers, you need to understand the journey that brought them here. That's the part they don't always realise they're ready to share — but it's where everything meaningful begins.

Where the Story Truly Begins

Before you share your advice, listen to their story.

Storytelling is a two-way street. Before we ever share our insights or offer guidance, we must first listen—truly listen—to our client's story. Who are they? Where have they come from? What moments have shaped them? It's in these personal narratives that the real work begins.

Clients like to tell their story—not just because it's cathartic, but because it helps them feel seen and valued. In a world that often rushes to offer solutions, being invited to share who they are and how they got here builds a rare kind of trust. It also gives advisers something more powerful than a fact-find ever could: context, emotion, and connection.

Too often, discovery meetings dive straight into financial concerns—budgets, pensions, fears about running out of money. But this approach can unintentionally trigger what psychologists call the Negative Emotional Attractor (NEA)—a state of stress and anxiety linked to problem-solving, risk aversion, and fear.

Consider John, who arrived at my office requesting "retirement planning." His body language spoke volumes—shoulders tensed, answers clipped, enthusiasm nowhere to be found. Rather than pulling out calculators or pension projections, I asked about his journey. It turned out John had poured 40 years into building a small manufacturing business. What the numbers couldn't reveal was that this wasn't just his livelihood, it was his community, his purpose, his very identity.

When he shared stories about mentoring young employees and solving unique production challenges, his entire demeanour changed. His eyes brightened, his posture relaxed, and suddenly we were having a completely different conversation. What he actually needed wasn't a standard retirement plan, but a transition strategy that kept him connected to the business while gradually stepping back. By hearing his story first, we designed a phased exit that protected his financial needs while preserving the aspects of work that gave his life meaning.

Or take David, who described himself as "extremely conservative" with investments. On paper, his caution seemed oddly misaligned with his successful career launching startups. The disconnect made sense only after he shared his childhood story of watching his parents lose everything in a financial crisis.

Rather than pushing him toward investments that matched his entrepreneurial profile, I acknowledged his lived experience. We developed a dual-track approach: a rock-solid secure foundation that addressed his emotional need for safety, alongside a smaller allocation for growth opportunities that honoured his business instincts. By respecting the story behind his risk aversion, we created a plan he could follow instead of one he would abandon at the first market downturn.

These examples highlight why we should begin by asking about the person behind the numbers. Invite them to explore the life they'd love to live. What does fulfilment look like to them? What hopes and dreams still feel possible?

This shift activates what behavioural experts call the Positive Emotional Attractor (PEA)—a more open, hopeful state of mind where clients feel energised, engaged, and optimistic. And as they begin to feel safe, heard, and inspired, something remarkable happens: the foundation for real, lasting financial planning is built.

So, before you ever open a spreadsheet or talk about risk, open the floor to their story. Let them feel seen. Let them feel heard. That's where the best financial journeys begin—and where your story, as their trusted adviser, truly starts.

Join me on this journey to master the art of financial storytelling, transforming technical expertise into your greatest asset in client relationships. Embrace clarity, connection, and the compelling power of narrative. Dive in!

CHAPTER 1

The Noble Art of Empowering Clients: Building Foundations for Financial Success

---◆---

"Tell me and I forget, teach me and I may remember, involve me and I learn."
—*Xunzi*

Early in my career, I thought being a good adviser meant knowing the numbers, building the spreadsheets, and presenting flawless, logical plans. I believed that if everything added up, the client would understand — and act.

But one meeting changed everything.

She sat across from me, arms folded tight, nodding politely. But her eyes? Miles away.

I'd just walked her through a pension forecast — the charts, the illustration, the spreadsheets, even the 32-page suitability report. Everything was correct. Everything made sense. And yet... nothing was landing. I could feel it — the moment where trust hangs in the balance. That quiet gap between logic and belief.

So, I closed the folder. Paused. Then simply said: "Can I tell you about someone I worked with who felt exactly like you — and the decision she made that changed everything?"

That was the moment her body shifted. She leaned in. Her expression softened. Her mind opened. For the first time in the meeting, she wasn't being advised — she was being understood.

And that's when it hit me:

Stories aren't just for marketing. They're the bridge between information and action. They're how clients make sense of complexity — and how we earn the right to be heard.

That story did something the data couldn't. It connected. It calmed. It clarified. Does this sound familiar? Have you ever sat in a client meeting where everything was factually right, but emotionally off?

That moment became a turning point for me. It was my lightbulb moment — the realisation that storytelling wasn't a soft skill or a nice-to-have. It was essential.

From that point on, I began to use stories with intention. Stories to simplify complexity. Stories to build trust. Stories to help clients feel seen and involved in their plan. And that's what this book is about. Because good advice isn't just what we say — it's what clients feel when we say it. And stories — real, relevant, human stories — are how we help them feel understood.

The Transformation of Financial Communication

Imagine a world where financial advice isn't a bewildering maze of numbers and jargon, but a clear, compelling journey of understanding. This is the promise of true financial storytelling— a profound art that transforms complex concepts into meaningful human experiences.

As a financial adviser, your role extends far beyond number crunching and investment selection. You are a navigator, a translator, a guide who helps clients traverse the often-overwhelming landscape of financial decision-making. Yet for too long, many advisers have struggled to bridge the critical gap between financial knowledge and genuine client understanding.

This book is not about tricks or manipulation. Storytelling in financial advisory isn't about persuasion for persuasion's sake. It's about empowerment—helping clients see, feel, and truly grasp financial concepts in a way that inspires confident action.

One powerful approach that embodies this philosophy of empowerment through storytelling is George Kinder's Three Questions methodology, which transforms financial conversations from transactional to deeply meaningful.

The Heart of Financial Storytelling: Beyond Numbers to Narrative

Most financial advisers begin their client meetings with numbers—assets, liabilities, pension balances, tax strategies. The spreadsheets appear, risk assessments are discussed, and products are proposed. But in this rush to analyse and solve, we often miss a more fundamental question: Why is this person really sitting across from us?

What truly drives our clients isn't just money. It's what money represents—security, freedom, purpose, legacy, or even unspoken fears about the future. These deeper motivations can't be captured in a cashflow projection or a risk profile questionnaire. They emerge through stories—the narratives clients tell about their past, their present concerns, and their hopes for tomorrow.

As financial advisers, our role transcends simply managing wealth or recommending products. Our true calling is to help clients craft a compelling vision for their lives and build a financial framework that enables them to live that vision. In this sacred space between dreams and financial reality, storytelling becomes not just valuable but essential.

The Three Questions That Transform Financial Conversations

Few approaches have been more transformative in interactions with clients than George Kinder's Three Questions. Widely regarded as the father of Life Planning, Kinder developed a deceptively simple methodology that shifts financial advice from transactional to deeply personal. His philosophy centres on the belief that people don't simply need money management—they need a meaningful narrative for their financial journey.

When I incorporate these questions into initial client conversations, the atmosphere in the room changes palpably. Shoulders relax, voices soften, and clients begin to speak from a place of authentic longing rather than financial anxiety:

Question One: "If you had all the money you needed—enough that you'd never have to worry about finances again—how would you live your life?"

This question removes constraints and invites clients to dream freely. I've watched the most analytically minded professionals transform as they describe sailing adventures, writing novels, teaching disadvantaged children, or simply having unhurried breakfasts with loved ones each morning.

Question Two: "If you learned you had only five to ten years to live, but would remain healthy until the very end, what would change? How would you live those years?"

This question introduces urgency and reveals priorities that suddenly become non-negotiable. I remember a client whose stoic demeanour cracked as he admitted he'd been postponing reconciliation with his estranged brother for "someday" that never seemed to arrive.

Question Three: "If you discovered you had just 24 hours to live, what would you regret? What did you miss? Who did you not get to be? What did you not get to do?"

This final question cuts to the essence of a client's values and often reveals profound truths. One particularly successful business owner broke down in tears, confessing she'd built significant wealth but had never allowed herself to enjoy it—always deferring happiness to a future that constantly receded before her.

Navigating the Discomfort of Mortality Conversations

Let's address the elephant in the room: these questions—particularly the second and third—require clients to confront their own mortality, a subject that many find deeply uncomfortable. As advisers, we too may hesitate to broach these topics, fearing we might upset clients or push them into emotional territory they aren't prepared to navigate.

This discomfort is entirely natural. Our society generally avoids direct conversations about death and finite time, and the financial profession has traditionally focused on growth and accumulation rather than meaning and purpose. Yet it is precisely this discomfort that signals we're approaching something of profound importance.

When introducing these questions, I've found several approaches helpful:

1. **Acknowledge the difficulty upfront:** "I'm going to ask you some questions that might feel challenging or even uncomfortable. They're designed to help us understand what truly matters to you beyond the numbers. We can take our time with them, and there are no right or wrong answers."

2. **Create psychological safety:** Ensure the environment is private and free from interruptions. Be comfortable with silence after asking the questions, allowing clients the space to process their thoughts without rushing to fill the void.

3. **Offer alternatives:** For clients who find direct mortality questions too confronting, try softening the approach: "What experiences or accomplishments would you most regret missing if life took an unexpected turn?" This often leads to the same insights without explicitly referencing death.

4. **Provide time for reflection:** Some of the most thoughtful responses come after clients have had time to consider these profound questions. I often say, "These questions touch on deeply personal matters. You're welcome to take them home and reflect on them before our next meeting. Sometimes the most valuable insights emerge when you're not put on the spot." This approach respects clients' emotional boundaries while still inviting meaningful engagement with the questions.

5. **Share the purpose:** Explain that these questions aren't merely philosophical exercises but have practical implications for how their financial plan will be structured. "Understanding what matters most to you helps us prioritise your resources accordingly."

6. **Be prepared for emotion:** Keep tissues available and be comfortable with clients expressing deep feelings. A client who tears up isn't having a bad experience—they're having an authentic one that will likely lead to more meaningful planning outcomes.

I've witnessed advisers skip these questions because they feel uncomfortable or unprepared to handle the emotions they might evoke. But in doing so, they miss the opportunity to transform a transactional relationship into a truly impactful partnership.

One adviser confided to me: "The first time I asked a client the '24 hours to live' question, I was terrified. But when he answered, describing how he'd spent decades building a business he didn't enjoy while missing his children's formative years, it changed everything. We restructured his entire financial plan to facilitate a business exit within 18 months rather than the 5-7 years we'd originally discussed. Three years later, he told me it was the most important conversation of his life."

The power of these questions lies in how they shift the conversation from financial products to life purposes. They transform clients from passive recipients of technical advice into active authors of their own financial stories.

The Adviser as Story Listener and Storyteller

When we pose these questions, most clients don't respond with financial objectives. Instead, they tell stories—about the business they've always dreamed of starting, the grandchildren they hope to take on once-in-a-lifetime adventures, or simply their vision of spending their final years in a cottage by the sea.

Our role as advisers is twofold: first, to listen deeply to these stories, recognising them as the true foundation of any meaningful financial plan; and second, to reflect these narratives back in a way that connects their dreams to concrete financial strategies.

The Oldest Story in Finance: What Stoics Teach Us About Clients Today

Long before we had platforms, models, and performance metrics, the deepest truths about client behaviour were already being explored—not in finance textbooks, but in the reflections of ancient philosophers. And while you won't find Marcus Aurelius mentioned in compliance training, his private journals hold surprising insights into how people make decisions under stress. In many ways, the challenges our clients face today—uncertainty, fear, identity, meaning—aren't new at all.

They're simply financial versions of timeless human questions.

This matters because when we talk about storytelling, we're not talking about fluff. We're talking about how humans have always made sense of uncertainty. And for advisers who want to elevate their conversations from transactional to transformational, it's worth borrowing from the thinkers who've been guiding human decisions for thousands of years.

But let's be clear—this isn't about quoting ancient wisdom to sound clever. It's about recognising that the stories clients bring to our meetings—*I don't want to make the same mistake again, I need to protect my family, I don't know who I'll be when I retire*—are age-old fears in modern packaging.

Let's explore a few examples.

> **"You have power over your mind—not outside events."** — Marcus Aurelius

When clients panic during a market crash, it's rarely the drop that causes distress—it's the feeling of losing control. Marcus Aurelius wrote about this during war, plague, and political chaos, reminding himself to focus on internal stability rather than external chaos.

For us, that means helping clients shift the story from *I'm at the mercy of the market* to *I can control how I respond*. One of the most powerful questions we can ask is:

"What would it look like to respond calmly if this happened again?"

You're not just offering perspective. You're handing them back the pen to rewrite the narrative.

> ***"It's not what happens to you, but how you react to it that matters."* — Epictetus**

Epictetus wasn't wealthy. In fact, he was born into slavery. But he became one of the most powerful voices on perspective. His lesson is simple: facts matter, but meaning matters more.

We see this play out when clients fixate on a poor investment choice from years ago. They often carry shame, fear, or embarrassment—until someone helps them rewrite that chapter as experience, not failure.

Try saying:

"You made a decision with the information you had at the time. What would you do differently now, and what does that tell us about how much you've grown?"

You're not changing the outcome—you're changing the story they tell about it.

> *"The whole future lies in uncertainty: live immediately."* — *Seneca*

Clients crave certainty—but financial life is anything but. Seneca's reminder wasn't to ignore the future, but to stop pretending it can be predicted.

That's why a good adviser doesn't promise certainty. They prepare clients for what life may throw their way. Storytelling here is about preparation, not prediction.

You might say:

"Let's imagine a few different futures. What would you want your story to be in each of them?"

Now you're helping them live with uncertainty, not fear it.

> *"The unexamined life is not worth living."*
> —*Socrates*

Socrates asked more questions than he gave answers—and that's why his conversations changed lives.

As advisers, we often feel pressure to lead with insight. But the best client conversations begin with curiosity. Before showing charts or plans, ask:

"What do you want your money to do for you?"
"What are you most proud of financially—and why?"

The answers may surprise you. More importantly, they guide you toward the real story behind the spreadsheet.

"Those who tell the stories rule society." — Plato

Plato understood that stories shape identity. And in our world, they shape behaviour. A client who believes "I'm bad with money" will make very different decisions than one who believes "I've learned to handle money with care."

Your job isn't to tell a perfect story. It's to help your client recognise the one they're already living—and gently offer them a better version.

Timeless Truths for Modern Advisers

Here's the bottom line: these philosophers weren't advisers—but they were students of human behaviour. They understood that logic alone rarely changes minds. Stories do. Especially the ones we tell ourselves.

You don't need to quote Marcus or Seneca in client meetings. But by embedding their timeless lessons into how you ask, listen, and guide, you bring something deeply human into your role—clarity, calm, and the wisdom to help clients make choices they'll be proud of later.

And in an industry flooded with noise, that's the kind of advice they'll never forget.

These timeless lessons remind us that storytelling is more than a communication tool—it's a way to align with human nature. But how do we apply that wisdom in the everyday decisions our clients face? That begins with how we translate strategy into a story.

Instead of saying, "Based on your risk profile, I recommend a balanced portfolio with a 60/40 equity-bond split," you might say:

"You've shared how important it is for you to retire early to spend more time with your family and travel while you're still active and healthy. Let's structure your financial plan to make that possible, ensuring you have both the freedom to explore and the security to enjoy that freedom without worry."

Similarly, when a client maintains an overly cautious investment approach that might undermine their long-term goals, a story becomes more powerful than statistics:

"Imagine it's fifteen years from now. Your grandson has been accepted to university, and you've always dreamed of helping with his education. But because you took such a cautious approach with your investments—keeping most of your money in cash and low-yielding bonds—your savings have barely kept pace with inflation. Now you're faced with an impossible choice: either watch your grandson defer his dreams or return to work yourself at 72 to help fund his education. After decades of hoping for a peaceful retirement, you find yourself back in the workforce not by choice, but by necessity. How would that scenario feel compared to taking a slightly more balanced approach to investing today?"

This approach to storytelling transforms financial planning from an abstract exercise into a deeply personal journey that clients can visualise, feel, and commit to with genuine conviction.

Creating Space for Reflection

The discomfort these questions may initially cause can actually serve a valuable purpose. By giving clients permission to sit with that discomfort—perhaps even sending the questions in advance so they can reflect privately before discussing them—we allow deeper truths to emerge.

One technique I've found effective is to frame these questions within the context of regret prevention. I often tell clients, "The three saddest phrases I've ever heard from clients are 'if only', 'I wish', and 'one day'. These questions help us ensure your financial plan doesn't leave room for those regrets." This approach helps clients understand that while discussing mortality may feel uncomfortable, the alternative—living with unaddressed regrets—is far more painful in the long run.

When clients grasp that these questions serve as a protective measure against future regret, they're often more willing to engage with them honestly and deeply. The temporary discomfort of confronting mortality pales in comparison to the lasting comfort of knowing their financial decisions align with their deepest values and aspirations.

Being There When It Matters Most

Clients don't pay us to be there all the time. They pay us to be there when they need us most—during life transitions, market turmoil, or when facing difficult financial decisions.

A financial plan built around these three profound questions is not simply about making numbers add up—it's about ensuring that when life takes unexpected turns, we can guide clients back to the vision they've established for themselves. We become keepers of their story, reminding them of what matters most when external circumstances threaten to distract or derail them.

For us as advisers, the challenge is clear: we must step beyond the comfortable territory of investment returns and tax strategies to become the storytellers who help clients see their future clearly, navigate their present wisely, and reconcile their past compassionately. By understanding their motivations at the deepest level, we do more than provide financial advice—we help them write the most important chapters of their lives, ensuring they have both the resources and the resolve to live their story fully.

In embracing the discomfort that comes with these profound conversations, we unlock the true potential of financial advice—not merely to grow wealth, but to nurture wellbeing, purpose, and meaning. When handled with sensitivity and skill, these difficult discussions become the foundation of true lifestyle financial planning, where money serves life rather than the other way around.

In the chapters that follow, we'll explore practical techniques for incorporating storytelling into every aspect of your financial advisory practice, from initial meetings to ongoing communications. But remember that all effective financial storytelling begins with this fundamental shift: from seeing clients as portfolios to manage to recognising them as stories unfolding.

The Essence of Memorable Teaching

Think about the most extraordinary teachers and speakers you've encountered. What made them remarkable? They didn't simply present facts. They painted vivid pictures with their words. They told stories that made lessons not just memorable, but real. This is the essence of storytelling, and it is the key to becoming an exceptional financial adviser.

The Primal Power of Narrative

Let me illustrate the pure, elemental power of storytelling. Imagine you're walking through the Arctic. Bitter cold surrounds you, snow swirling, your boots crunching on crisp ice. Suddenly, a polar bear appears—and it sees you. It starts running toward you.

In that precise moment, grammatical analysis becomes irrelevant. You don't dissect nouns or parse verbs. Your mind instantaneously creates a vivid mental movie. You feel the raw fear, the immediate survival instinct. This is how stories work. They bypass intellectual barriers and speak directly to our most fundamental understanding.

This visceral response to narrative isn't limited to survival scenarios—it permeates our everyday experiences. Take song lyrics, for example. ABBA's Dancing Queen opens with "Friday night and the lights are low." Instantly, you're placed in a scene, feeling the atmosphere. Lyrics tell stories that evoke emotions, transporting us back to moments in time. Financial advisers must do the same—using stories to anchor abstract concepts in clients' minds in a way that resonates emotionally.

Financial Foundations: More Than Just Numbers

Financial decisions are remarkably like building a house. A weak foundation dooms even the most elegant design. The choices clients make early—about saving, investing, managing risk—are the cornerstone of their financial future. Poor decisions, made from ignorance or fear, can create long-term instabilities that become increasingly difficult to rectify.

Financial concepts are often abstract, filled with intimidating jargon, and disconnected from everyday experience. Data, graphs, and reports might provide clarity to an adviser, but they rarely inspire meaningful action in clients. This is precisely where storytelling becomes not just useful, but essential.

The Professional Metamorphosis: Storytelling as a Career Catalyst

Mastering financial storytelling is more than a communication skill—it's a professional differentiator that can fundamentally transform your advisory practice. In an era of algorithm-driven investments and digital platforms, the human capacity to create meaningful narratives becomes your most powerful competitive advantage.

Advisers who excel at storytelling:

- Build deeper, more trusting client relationships
- Increase client retention rates
- Attract more referrals through memorable experiences
- Simplify complex financial concepts
- Empower clients to make more confident decisions

This is not just about being a better communicator. It's about becoming a financial guide who can truly illuminate paths forward, transforming technical knowledge into actionable, inspiring insights.

The Emotional Landscape of Financial Choices

Here's a fundamental truth: emotions drive decisions far more powerfully than logic. This is especially true in financial matters, where fear, greed, anxiety, and overconfidence often dictate choices. When advisers rely solely on numbers and statistics, they miss a critical opportunity to connect with clients on a deeply human level.

Consider two approaches to explaining the importance of staying invested during market downturns:

Logical Approach: "The S&P 500 has historically rebounded after every downturn, making long-term investing the statistically superior choice."

Story-Driven Approach: "I once had a client who panicked during the 2008 financial crisis and wanted to sell everything. We talked through their concerns, and they decided to stay the course. A decade later, their portfolio had doubled."

Both statements are factually accurate. But only one creates an emotional connection that can truly motivate action.

From Abstract to Tangible: A Visual Journey of Understanding

Sometimes, the most powerful stories aren't just told—they're demonstrated. Let me show you how a simple visual metaphor can transform a complex financial concept into a moment of pure clarity.

The Two-Beaker Financial Journey: Understanding Stocks and Bonds

Let's clear up a common misconception. Most people with an investment Individual Savings Account (ISA) or personal pension often assume they're fully invested in the stock market. But that's not entirely accurate. While it's true they are 100% invested, it doesn't mean all their money is in the stock market—or, as I prefer to call it, the great companies of the world, which is what the stock market truly represents.

Picture this: Two crystal-clear beakers stand before you, each telling a story of financial possibility. They're not just containers—they're windows into the very nature of investment.

Setting the Stage

I place the first beaker in front of you. "This," I say, "is the world of stocks." The second beaker sits alongside it, a quieter companion. "And this? This is the world of bonds."

Both beakers are precisely marked, vertical lines climbing from 0 to 100, each increment a testament to potential. But potential comes in different flavours.

I begin to pour. Clear liquid—representing your hard-earned money—cascades into each beaker. Sixty per cent flows into the stocks beaker, a focused, purposeful stream, symbolising the pursuit of long-term growth. Forty per cent settles into the bonds beaker, more measured, more restrained.

The Dance of Volatility

"Watch closely," I say, and gently tilt the stocks beaker.

Suddenly, the liquid comes alive. It's not just moving—it's dancing, leaping, unpredictable. One moment calm, the next surging toward the top of the beaker's sides. This is volatility embodied. Each shake creates waves, some small, some dramatic. The liquid seems to have a personality—energetic, sometimes wild, full of potential.

Now, look closely. Because there's more liquid in the stocks beaker, there's more surface area for movement. More liquid means more potential for those dramatic ups and downs. When I shake the beaker, more of the liquid rises and falls against the glass—that's volatility in action.

The bonds beaker tells a different story. I apply a gentler movement, and something remarkable happens. Barely a ripple. With less liquid in the beaker, there's simply less that can move. Less to be volatile. It's stability personified.

"This," I explain, "is the fundamental trade-off of investing. Higher potential returns come with higher movement. Lower potential returns offer less movement and more stability."

A Living Metaphor

As I continue to tilt and shake the stocks beaker, the liquid's behaviour becomes a narrative. Sometimes it climbs high, promising exciting growth. Sometimes it retreats, hinting at potential losses. But always, there's movement. Always, there's possibility.

The bonds beaker sits in quiet contrast. Stable. Predictable. A harbour of calm amid the stocks' stormy sea.

The Balancing Act

I demonstrate what happens when we adjust the mix. More stocks? More liquid, more movement. Less liquid in bonds? Less stability. More stocks? More potential for both growth and drops. It's not about choosing between excitement and boredom—it's about finding your client's personal financial rhythm.

"Imagine," I say, "this is your financial journey. Some people want a rollercoaster. Some want a gentle river cruise. Most want something in between."

Beyond the Beakers

This isn't just about liquids and glass. It's about understanding that investing isn't a guarantee, it's a carefully navigated path. The stocks beaker represents the great companies of the world, their potential for growth, their capacity for innovation. The bonds beaker represents stability, reliability, the steady heartbeat of your financial security.

The Long-Term Story of Ownership

Here's a curious thought experiment. Imagine stopping 100 people on the street and asking a simple question: "Would you rather own a small piece of companies like Microsoft, Apple, or

Amazon—or lend them money?" Most would light up at the ownership idea. They'd talk about these remarkable businesses they use every single day. The phones in their pockets, the computers on their desks, the services that connect their world.

Yet, paradoxically, many of these same people shy away from the stock market—those very same great companies—because the words "stock market" sound intimidating. They'll happily use an iPhone, but the idea of owning a piece of Apple becomes somehow scary.

The historical evidence is compelling. While there are absolutely no guarantees, patient long-term investors who have owned pieces of the world's great businesses have significantly outperformed those who simply lent money to these businesses through bonds. It's not even close. Over decades, stocks have dramatically outpaced bonds, rewarding those with the patience to ride out the volatility we saw in our beakers.

Think of it this way: Would you rather be the person who lends money to a business and receives a small, fixed return? Or the part-owner who shares in the business's actual growth, innovations, and success? The beakers tell that story. More movement, yes. More potential, absolutely.

The liquid in the stocks beaker isn't just moving—it's representing the dynamic, innovative spirit of human enterprise. Those waves and fluctuations? They're the sound of businesses growing, adapting, creating value. It's what the disrupters do. The bonds beaker might be calm, but calm doesn't build the technologies that change the world.

The Human Element

As I set the beakers down, something magical happens. Clients see. Really see. The abstract becomes tangible. Volatility is no longer a scary financial term—it's that liquid dancing against the glass. Stability isn't boring—it's a peaceful reassurance.

"Remember," I say, "this isn't about predicting the future. This is about understanding the journey."

And just like that, a complex financial concept becomes a story. A story they can see, touch, understand.

Your Journey Through This Book

As you progress through these pages, you'll discover a comprehensive storytelling framework designed specifically for financial advisers:

- **Chapter 2-3**: Foundational storytelling techniques and narrative structures
- **Chapter 4-5**: Creating relatable characters and setting powerful contexts
- **Chapter 6-7**: Simplifying complex concepts and building client trust
- **Chapter 8-9**: Advanced engagement strategies across different communication platforms
- **Chapter 10-11**: Practical case studies and ethical considerations
- **Chapter 12-13**: Developing your personal storytelling toolkit and measuring impact

Each chapter builds upon the last, creating a holistic approach to financial narrative mastery. You're not just learning a skill, you're developing a transformative professional philosophy.

The Snake in the Glass Box: Emotion Overrides Logic

Picture a sealed glass box on a table. Inside, a large snake coils motionless. You lean in, curious. Suddenly, it rears up, striking toward the glass. Instinctively, you jump back.

Logically, you know the glass provides protection. But your brain reacts before logic can intervene. Why? Because our emotional responses are hard-wired to override rational analysis, especially when survival instincts are triggered.

Financial decisions follow an identical psychological pattern. Clients might logically understand that staying invested is the rational choice, but their emotional instincts—fears of loss, anxieties about uncertainty—can drive them to make fundamentally irrational decisions.

Your role as an adviser transcends merely providing information. You must counteract fear with understanding, replace uncertainty with confidence. And storytelling is your most powerful tool in achieving this transformation.

The Crystal Ball: A Lesson in Financial Honesty

Whenever I meet clients for the first time, there's always something sitting on the table that grabs their attention immediately—a small crystal ball, about the size of a tennis ball. It's not there by accident. Strategic. Deliberate. A conversation waiting to happen.

As my client settles into the chair, I casually reach for it, a hint of theatrical resignation in my movement. "Oh, sorry—I meant to remove this before you came in," I say, my tone a perfect blend of mild embarrassment and comic timing. "It's the 67th one I've tried... and unfortunately, this one doesn't work either."

Without fail, it gets a laugh. A tension-breaking, wall-lowering laugh that transforms the entire mood of the meeting.

But beneath the humour lies a serious point sharper than any financial projection. I don't have a crystal ball that works. I cannot predict the future, and I'd be deeply suspicious of anyone who claims they can. Markets will rise. Markets will fall. Returns will fluctuate. These are the immutable truths of investing.

This light-hearted moment carries profound meaning. It establishes trust through three powerful ingredients: honesty, humility, and a touch of self-deprecating humour. In one simple gesture, I've made myself human. Memorable.

When markets inevitably suffer their temporary dips—and they will—this moment becomes an anchor. "Remember the crystal ball?" I'll say, and instantly, they'll recall our first meeting. They'll remember we always knew uncertainty was part of the journey.

It's more than an ice breaker. It's a philosophy of financial advising distilled into a single, memorable moment. No predictions. No false promises. Just genuine partnership.

The crystal ball sits quietly, a silent reminder: the future isn't something to be predicted, but a journey to be navigated together.

Of course, this particular approach might not suit your own personality or communication style—and that's perfectly fine. The point isn't to necessarily copy the gimmick; it's to find your version of it. Something unexpected, authentic, and a little different from your peers that leaves a lasting impression. In a world of forgettable meetings and generic advice, being memorable is a competitive advantage.

From Accepting Uncertainty to Managing It

While the crystal ball acknowledges what we cannot control—the unpredictable nature of markets—clients still need guidance on what they can control: their attention and response to market events. This is where another powerful visual metaphor enters the conversation, addressing the constant barrage of financial media that often derails even the most disciplined investors.

The Noise-Cancelling Headphones: Tuning Out the Market Madness

Another powerful visual prop that creates an immediate client connection is a pair of premium noise-cancelling headphones. Like the crystal ball, these become a tangible metaphor that transforms abstract financial concepts into something clients can literally see and touch.

You lift them up during your client meeting, turning them slowly in your hands. "Have you ever worn a pair of these on a crowded flight?"

You wait for their reaction, then continue. "What makes these remarkable isn't just that they block sound—it's that they're selective about what they block."

You place them gently on the table. "These headphones use sophisticated technology to identify disruptive noise—the roar of jet engines, the chatter of passengers, crying babies—and then generate precise counter-frequencies that neutralise only those sounds. The important announcements? The conversation with your seatmate? Those still come through clearly."

You slide their financial plan across the table. "A well-designed financial strategy works the same way. It doesn't shut out all market information—just the disruptive noise that adds no value:

the daily market predictions, the latest investment fads and hot tips, the panic-inducing headlines."

You open the plan to their long-term goals page. "This is what you should be listening to—your retirement timeline, your children's education, your legacy goals. When the market starts screaming, your plan creates those counter-frequencies, allowing you to hear only what truly deserves your attention."

Picking up the headphones again, you press the power button. "The best part? Once you put these on, you don't have to actively fight to ignore the noise. The technology does that work for you. Similarly, once we establish your plan, it handles the noise-cancellation automatically, letting you enjoy the journey without constant disruption."

In a world designed to profit from your emotional reactions, a thoughtful financial plan acts as your personal noise-cancellation system, filtering out market madness while keeping you tuned in to what actually matters for your financial future.

The False Prophets: A Storytelling Opportunity

In today's fast-paced and ever-changing financial landscape, individuals are bombarded with a constant stream of advice and predictions from so-called financial experts in the media. Clients often tell me about something they read or saw on television. These self-proclaimed gurus, armed with charts, graphs, and compelling narratives, portray themselves as the key to unlocking financial success.

However, a closer examination reveals a stark truth: if these experts were truly as accurate as they claim, they would have long retired to enjoy a life of leisure on a beach in the Bahamas. The fact that they continue to draft articles for a living rather than having the courage and conviction to fully invest based on their own predictions raises legitimate questions about the value of their advice. After all, if they truly believed in their forecasts with unwavering conviction, wouldn't their own investment success have made publishing financial opinions unnecessary?

As economist John Kenneth Galbraith astutely observed, "There are two kinds of forecasters: those who don't know, and those who don't know they don't know."

Morgan Housel, the insightful author of "The Psychology of Money," speaks to this very human preoccupation with predicting future outcomes: "The inability to forecast the past has no impact on our desire to forecast the future." This observation cuts to the heart of our relationship with financial uncertainty. We all want answers. The problem is there aren't any, especially about the short term.

It simply doesn't matter what the fundamental or technical analysis says or what analysts and pundits predict, because anything is possible in the short term. This has always been the case and always will be, which is why timing the market remains impossible.

In the long term, history suggests that markets will generally follow earnings just as they've done for the last century. But in the short run, anything can happen.

This presents a perfect storytelling opportunity for advisers. When clients come to you influenced by the latest market prediction or hot investment tip, you can counter these forecasters not with competing predictions, but with compelling narratives about patience, perspective, and historical context. Your stories become the antidote to the poison of short-term thinking—a way to reconnect clients with their actual financial journey rather than the illusory shortcuts promised by financial media.

Consider crafting a simple story about two hypothetical investors: one who followed every market prediction and hot tip for a decade, and another who stayed committed to a thoughtful, long-term plan regardless of market noise. The ending writes itself, and the moral becomes clear without preaching. This narrative approach transforms the abstract concept of "ignoring market predictions" into a tangible lesson clients can visualise and remember when the next market guru appears on their television screen.

The client response to this storytelling approach is often remarkable. You can see the moment of clarity dawn in their expression—a mixture of relief and understanding. "I never thought about it that way," they'll often say, their shoulders visibly relaxing. Some will laugh, recognising how they've been swayed by the very forecasters you've described. "You're right—if they knew what was coming, why would they tell everyone?" Others nod thoughtfully, making the connection to their own behaviour:

This moment of realisation is precisely why storytelling transcends traditional financial advice. You haven't simply told them to ignore market predictions—you've helped them see for themselves why such predictions are fundamentally flawed. The story becomes their own insight; one they've discovered rather than been lectured about. And discoveries we make ourselves are the ones we truly remember and act upon.

The Ripple Effect: Stories Beyond Individual Interactions

Effective storytelling extends far beyond individual client meetings. It has the potential to:

- Reshape organisational culture within financial advisory firms
- Create more inclusive, accessible financial education
- Challenge traditional, jargon-heavy communication approaches
- Empower clients to become more financially literate and confident

Your stories have the power to change not just individual financial journeys, but potentially the entire landscape of financial communication.

Crafting Stories for Different Clients

Not every client responds to the same narrative approach. The key to effective storytelling is identifying individual personality types and communication styles:

- The Analytical Thinker requires case studies and logic-driven explanations
- The Emotional Decision-Maker connects through human-centred stories
- The Sceptical Client benefits from contrast-based narratives that demonstrate different investment approaches

Decoding Client Communication Styles: The Pre-Meeting Detective Work

Becoming a masterful financial storyteller begins long before you sit across from your client. It starts with strategic research and intelligent information gathering that allows you to tailor your narrative approach from the first moment of interaction.

Digital Footprint Analysis

In today's interconnected world, clients leave behind a wealth of communication clues through their digital presence:

1. **Social Media Investigation**

   - LinkedIn profiles reveal professional language and communication preferences
   - Written posts show whether they prefer technical or emotional narratives
   - Professional achievements and language can indicate analytical tendencies

2. **Online Professional Profiles**

   - Academic backgrounds suggest communication style
   - Job roles often correlate with preferred information delivery
   - Published articles or comments demonstrate thinking patterns

Preliminary Questionnaire Techniques

Design a pre-meeting communication style assessment that subtly reveals preferences:

- Use short, strategic questions that provide insight
- Create scenarios that demonstrate communication preferences
- Include visual, numerical, and narrative-based response options
- Ensure the questionnaire feels engaging, not like an interrogation

Sample Pre-Meeting Communication Profiling Questions:

"When making a significant decision, which approach resonates most with you?

A) A detailed spreadsheet with comprehensive data

B) A story about someone who successfully navigated a similar situation

C) A comparative analysis showing multiple potential outcomes"

Referral and Network Intelligence

Leverage your professional network for insights:

- Speak with the referring contact about the client's communication style
- Request introductory background information
- Ask subtle questions that reveal communication preferences

Preliminary Document Request Strategy

How a client responds to initial document requests can reveal volumes:

- An analytical thinker might provide meticulously organised financial records
- An emotional decision-maker might include personal context with their documents
- A sceptical client might ask numerous clarifying questions about the purpose of the documents

Telephone/Initial Consultation Techniques

Your first verbal interaction is a goldmine of communication style insights:

- Note the type of questions they ask
- Observe their language complexity
- Pay attention to whether they prefer concrete facts or broader perspectives
- Listen for emotional undertones or analytical precision

Technology-Assisted Profiling

Emerging AI and personality assessment tools can provide preliminary insights:

- Linguistic analysis software
- Advanced personality profiling platforms
- Communication style assessment algorithms

Red Flags and Nuanced Observations

Be aware that no single technique is foolproof. Always:

- Remain flexible in your approach
- Be prepared to adjust your narrative style in real-time
- Recognise that clients are complex, multifaceted individuals

The Adaptive Storyteller's Mindset

The goal isn't to categorise clients into rigid boxes, but to develop a nuanced, empathetic understanding that allows you to craft narratives that resonate on a deeply personal level. Think of yourself as a communication chameleon—able to adjust your storytelling palette to match each unique client's preferences.

Your ability to read, understand, and adapt becomes your most powerful advisory tool.

Remember, true mastery in financial storytelling isn't about having a perfect system. It's about cultivating an intuitive, adaptive approach that sees each client as a unique individual with their own narrative waiting to be understood.

The Architecture of a Compelling Story

Every powerful story follows a fundamental structure:

1. **The Problem:** A relatable financial challenge
2. **The Struggle:** The emotional and practical difficulties faced
3. **The Resolution:** Lessons learned through patience and discipline
4. **The Transformation:** The ultimate positive outcome of the financial journey

Before we close this first chapter, I want to share a simple but often overlooked truth. Financial storytelling isn't just about chasing bigger numbers — it's about safeguarding what matters most. And sometimes, the most important part of the story isn't what we're trying to grow — it's what we're trying to protect.

The Hidden Asset: Your Most Valuable Investment

The morning light filtered through the blinds of my office as Sarah settled into the chair across from my desk. It was our annual review meeting, and we'd just finished discussing her investment portfolio when I decided to broach a topic, she'd been reluctant to address in our previous sessions.

"Sarah," I began, "I'd like to ask you something a bit different today." I leaned forward slightly. "Imagine there was a machine in your home that reliably generated £3,000 every month without fail. Would you insure that machine?"

Sarah was silent for a moment, considering the question.

"Would I insure a machine that generates £3,000 every month without fail? Of course I would," she finally responded, leaning forward in her chair. "I'd be mad not to."

I smiled and placed my coffee cup on the table between us. "Then why haven't you insured yourself, Sarah?"

Her brow furrowed. "What do you mean?"

"That magical money-generating machine—it's sitting right here," I said, gesturing toward her. "It's you."

This conversation changed everything for Sarah. For years, she had meticulously insured her home, her car, even her pet labrador, Max. But she'd never seriously considered protecting her most valuable asset: her ability to earn.

As financial advisers, we often fall into a pattern of telling only half the story. We love discussing investment growth, market opportunities, and financial success—the sunny days of finance. And those stories matter. They inspire. They motivate.

But genuine financial storytelling requires a more complete narrative, one that acknowledges an uncomfortable truth: no asset in your client's portfolio is more valuable than their capacity to generate income. It's the engine that powers every financial dream they hold.

James, another client, once challenged me on this point.

"I don't like thinking about getting ill or being unable to work," he admitted during our annual review. "It feels... pessimistic."

I nodded. "James, do you remember when you told me about teaching your daughter to ride a bike?"

He smiled at the memory. "Of course."

"Did you put a helmet on her head because you expected her to fall, or because you wanted to protect what matters most if the unexpected happened?"

His expression softened with understanding.

"Protection isn't about pessimism," I continued. "It's about creating the freedom to be optimistic. It's ensuring that the dreams you're working so hard to build remain protected, no matter what life throws your way."

Last year, I conducted a simple experiment at a client seminar. I asked everyone in the room to raise their hand if they had critical illness cover. A few hesitant hands went up.

Then I posed a different question: "If you were guaranteed to survive a critical illness but knew with certainty it would happen to you, how many would buy protection right now?"

Every single hand shot up.

This reveals something profound about human psychology. We understand the rational case for protection, but emotionally, we distance ourselves from potential challenges. We're wired to focus on positive outcomes—blue skies and rising markets—while believing "it won't happen to me."

Yet deep down, we all know prevention is better than cure. We service our cars, get regular health check-ups, and maintain our homes. Why then, when it comes to protecting our most valuable asset—our ability to earn and create—do we hesitate?

The magic happens when we move beyond statistics and technical jargon to have conversations that feel like chats between friends, where complex ideas become simple truths. When we speak from a place of genuine concern rather than sales pressure, people don't just listen—they truly hear us.

Consider this approach: Sit down with your client, perhaps over a cup of tea, and say, "Let me help you see this from a different perspective."

Then tell them about the machine—the extraordinary device that generates thousands of pounds each month, funding everything they value. Help them see themselves as that irreplaceable asset. Ask them what would happen to all their carefully constructed financial plans if that machine suddenly stopped working.

When clients understand that financial planning isn't just about wealth accumulation but about protecting their capacity to create that wealth in the first place, everything changes. The conversation shifts from product-focused to purpose-driven.

Emma, a long-term client, once thanked me for "being persistent" about protection coverage years earlier. When a serious health condition forced her to take six months away from her business, that policy became the difference between financial stability and distress.

"You didn't just protect my income," she told me. "You protected my peace of mind. And that's been just as valuable."

This is our true calling as financial advisers: not merely to help clients accumulate wealth, but to safeguard their ability to create it. Not just to plan for sunny days, but to ensure they can weather any storm.

Because when we understand that the most valuable investment is the client themselves, we approach every financial conversation with greater meaning, purpose, and care.

And that's a story worth telling.

A Call to Financial Storytellers

You are more than an adviser. You are a teacher, a guide, and above all, a storyteller. The decisions your clients make today will shape their financial lives for decades to come. Your ability to frame those decisions in a compelling, memorable way will determine whether they take action—or stay paralysed by complexity and fear.

Here's your first challenge: In your very next client meeting, replace one data-heavy explanation with a carefully crafted story. Observe what happens. Do they lean in? Ask more questions? Show signs of clarity and confidence?

This book will give you the tools to master the noble art of financial storytelling. The transformation begins with you.

A Final Invitation

The journey ahead is more than a chance to refine your skills. It's an opportunity to reimagine financial advice—not as a transactional service, but as a human, story-led partnership.

Every great transformation begins with a single story.

Your story starts now.

10 KEY TAKEAWAYS

1. Financial storytelling is not about manipulation but empowerment—helping clients truly grasp financial concepts in a way that inspires confident action and better decision-making.

2. Storytelling transforms complex financial concepts into meaningful human experiences, making abstract ideas tangible and accessible to clients.

3. Emotions drive financial decisions far more powerfully than logic, making storytelling essential for addressing the true motivators of client behaviour.

4. Different client personality types require tailored narrative approaches—analytical thinkers, emotional decision-makers, and sceptical clients all respond to different storytelling techniques.

5. In an increasingly automated financial industry, the human ability to craft meaningful narratives becomes a powerful professional differentiator and competitive advantage.

6. Visual metaphors and storytelling techniques can transform complex financial concepts into clear, memorable experiences that clients can easily understand and relate to.

7. Honesty, humility, and a touch of humour are powerful tools in building trust and creating lasting connections with clients, transcending traditional financial advisory approaches.

8. Transformative techniques like Kinder's Three Questions help clients articulate their deepest values and priorities,

creating a foundation for meaningful financial planning that aligns with what truly matters to them.

9. Navigating difficult conversations about mortality requires sensitivity and skill, but when handled effectively, these discussions can prevent future regrets and ensure financial decisions support clients' most profound life aspirations.

10. True financial storytelling isn't just about growth — it's about protecting the foundations of every financial dream. Trusted advisers have the courage to raise important conversations clients might otherwise avoid, helping them safeguard their future with care and compassion.

CHAPTER 2

Understanding the Power of Stories

———◇———

"The human species thinks in metaphors and learns through stories."
—*Mary Catherine Bateson*

Rory Sutherland on the Power of Storytelling

Rory Sutherland, Vice Chairman of Ogilvy and one of the sharpest minds in behavioural economics, offers a compelling case for why storytelling matters more than logic when it comes to influencing human behaviour. In his book Alchemy, he explains that the most effective solutions often don't make rational sense—because human beings aren't purely rational. We're emotional, intuitive, meaning-driven. And that's where storytelling has its power.

When I came across Sutherland's work, it immediately resonated with what I've seen in financial advice. Clients rarely take action because of data points or charts. They move when something makes sense to them. When it feels right. When they can picture it. That's what a well-crafted story does. It builds a bridge between technical truth and emotional truth.

Sutherland often uses beautifully simple examples. He once said that instead of spending millions to reduce a train journey by five minutes, we could just make the journey more enjoyable—better coffee, comfortable seating, free Wi-Fi. People don't just want speed; they want experience. It's a perfect metaphor for advice. We spend so much time trying to optimise plans, but often what clients need is reassurance, understanding, and perspective.

His approach—challenging assumptions, reframing problems, and using counterintuitive insights—mirrors exactly how I believe good advisers should communicate. When we explain investment concepts or behavioural traps through story, we're not dumbing things down—we're making them human. And that's where real connection happens.

Ultimately, Sutherland reminds us of something essential: people don't just seek information. They seek meaning. And story is the most powerful way we can offer it.

Let me tell you why stories work so well: our brains are wired to remember them. Here's what you need to do. Stop bombarding your clients with facts and figures. Instead, weave those facts into a narrative. I've used the analogy of the stock market being like the tide. It goes out, but it always comes back in. Clients remember that much more than they would a technical explanation of volatility.

What is Storytelling in Financial Advisory?

Storytelling in financial advisory is the art of conveying financial concepts through narratives that resonate with your clients. It involves weaving data and strategies into stories that clients can relate to and remember, making the advice you offer more impactful and actionable. For example, instead of explaining compound interest in a technical way, you could describe it as a snowball rolling down a hill, gathering size and momentum as it goes. The visual and emotional impact of that story sticks far longer than a spreadsheet ever could.

The Psychology Behind Stories: Why They Work

Humans are wired for stories. From childhood, stories are how we learn and how we connect. They excite and inspire us and is how we make sense of the world. This innate preference for narratives has a profound psychological basis:

1. **Memory Retention:** Stories activate multiple parts of the brain, including those responsible for emotions, senses, and memory. This makes the information within a story far easier to recall than raw data.

2. **Emotional Engagement:** Facts appeal to logic, but stories appeal to emotions. When you tell a story, clients not only understand the concept but feel connected to it. This connection builds trust and helps clients see the relevance of your advice in their lives.

3. **Decision-Making:** Stories help bridge the gap between the rational and emotional parts of the brain. When clients are faced with complex financial decisions, stories can provide clarity by framing choices in a way that feels intuitive and less overwhelming.

Beyond Words: The Neuroscience of Narrative Power

Recent advances in neuroscience have unveiled the profound biological mechanisms that make storytelling such a powerful communication tool. When we hear a dry list of facts, only the language processing areas of our brain activate. But a compelling story? It creates a neurological symphony, lighting up regions responsible for emotions, sensory experiences, memory, and decision-making.

Stories resonate because they are more than just words—they are lived experiences. Functional MRI studies reveal something remarkable: our brains respond to stories almost identically to lived experiences. When a financial adviser tells a compelling story about overcoming economic challenges, the listener's brain doesn't just passively receive information. It actively reconstructs the experience, firing neurons as if the listener were living through the narrative themselves.

This process is largely driven by mirror neurons—specialised brain cells that allow us to empathise with others—which cause clients to experience a story as if they were living it themselves. When you tell a compelling story, clients aren't just hearing it; they're feeling it. This neurological mirroring creates a deep, almost visceral understanding that transcends traditional information transfer.

The brain's hormonal response further enhances this connection. When a story is compelling, our brain releases oxytocin, often called the "connection hormone," which fosters empathy, trust, and emotional engagement. This isn't just a feel-good response, it's a biological mechanism that builds trust, reduces anxiety, and opens the mind to new perspectives. This explains why a well-told story can be more persuasive than a thousand statistics and why clients will remember an analogy about compound interest growing like a snowball far more than a dry explanation of exponential growth rates.

The emotional pull of a story also triggers dopamine release, ensuring the lesson is not just understood but remembered. Dopamine, known as the "happy hormone," is released during pleasurable experiences and plays a crucial role in reinforcing learning.

Neuroplasticity offers an even more remarkable insight into storytelling's power. Each powerful narrative has the potential to reshape neural pathways, helping clients literally rewire their thinking about financial challenges. A story about financial resilience isn't just information—it's a potential blueprint for cognitive transformation. For financial advisers, this means a well-crafted story can literally change how a client perceives financial risk and opportunity.

Just like a powerful movie scene stays with you long after leaving the theatre, a well-told financial story stays with your client, shaping how they process financial decisions long after the conversation ends. This enduring impact is why storytelling isn't just a communication technique but a fundamental tool for transformative financial advice.

For financial advisers, these neurological insights are transformative. Your stories aren't just communication—they're a form of experiential learning that literally reshapes how clients perceive and interact with financial concepts, creating lasting change in both understanding and behaviour.

The History of Storytelling in Wealth and Finance

Storytelling has long been a tool for passing down financial wisdom, dating back to ancient times. Long before modern investment theories, societies relied on fables, myths, and oral traditions to teach financial prudence.

Ancient Money Myths: Lessons from the Past

In ancient Greece, Aesop's fables often held financial lessons like "The Ant and the Grasshopper," which warns against failing to save for the future. Similarly, ancient Chinese parables emphasised delayed gratification and resourcefulness, key principles in financial planning today.

Global Narratives: A Cultural Journey of Financial Wisdom

Financial storytelling is a universal language, yet each culture brings its unique dialect. In Japan, financial wisdom often emerges through concepts of collective responsibility and long-term thinking. Traditional Japanese stories frequently emphasise patience, modest living, and careful investment.

Indigenous Australian cultures offer profound narrative approaches to understanding value and exchange. Their storytelling traditions transform financial concepts into deeply meaningful journeys of community and sustainability. A story isn't just about money, it's about relationships, survival, and collective well-being.

West African oral traditions demonstrate how storytelling can encode complex economic principles. Intricate narratives about trade, community support, and resource management become living lessons passed through generations. These stories do more than teach—they preserve economic knowledge in a format that resonates deeply with human experience.

Consider how these diverse narrative approaches can enrich your financial storytelling:

- Embrace stories that highlight collective success
- Use metaphors that reflect cultural understanding of value
- Recognise that financial wisdom transcends numerical calculations

The Role of Storytelling in Banking & Investment

In the Middle Ages, money lenders and merchants used storytelling to build trust. Even today, legendary investors like Warren Buffett rely on simple, relatable narratives rather than complex financial jargon to connect with the public.

From Wall Street to Main Street

Large financial firms often craft narratives to shape public perception - think of the "safe haven" story behind gold or the "growth potential" story behind tech stocks. The power of storytelling has always influenced financial decision-making, making it a timeless and essential tool for advisers.

How Stories Bridge the Gap Between Data and Emotion

Data alone can be dry and difficult to digest. Stories infuse data with emotion, making it easier for clients to understand and relate to the financial concepts you are presenting. Consider this scenario: Instead of saying, "The market historically recovers after downturns," tell a story about a retired couple who stayed invested through the 2008 financial crisis and went on to enjoy a secure retirement. This narrative not only illustrates the concept but also provides a real-world example that clients can see themselves in.

Market Psychology and Pattern Recognition

Many people look to financial forecasters for guidance, believing that expert predictions can provide certainty in an uncertain world. However, just like the weather, financial markets are influenced by countless unpredictable factors, making precise forecasting incredibly difficult.

Analogy: Financial Forecasters Are Like the Weather - Unreliable

Relying on financial forecasters is like planning a picnic based on a long-term weather forecast. The forecast might say it'll be sunny, but a rainstorm could still appear out of nowhere. Just like the weather, markets are shaped by numerous variables — global events, investor sentiment, interest rates, and technological shifts — most of which are impossible to predict accurately. Forecasters can give you an idea of what might happen, but relying on them to perfectly predict the future is risky and unreliable. Instead, just like carrying an umbrella no matter what the forecast says, investors should be prepared for market ups and downs rather than banking on predictions.

Analogy: The Emotional Impact of Stories

Stories are not just a communication tool; they are a way to inspire action. When clients see themselves in the stories you share, they are more likely to follow through on your advice. By connecting their emotions to their financial goals, you help them make decisions with confidence and clarity.

The Art of Interactive Financial Storytelling

Storytelling is not a monologue—it's a dialogue. The most powerful narratives invite participation, creating a collaborative journey of understanding.

Interactive storytelling techniques:

- Pause at critical moments and ask clients, "What would you do in this situation?"
- Use open-ended questions that encourage personal reflection

- Create narrative frameworks where clients can insert their own experiences
- Develop stories with multiple potential paths, allowing client input

Imagine explaining investment diversification not as a lecture, but as an exploratory journey. "Let's imagine we're building a garden together. What plants would you choose to ensure a resilient harvest?" Suddenly, complex financial concepts become a shared adventure.

Technology and the Future of Financial Narratives

Digital platforms are transforming how we tell and experience stories. Artificial Intelligence offers unprecedented opportunities for personalised narrative creation. Imagine AI tools that can:

- Analyse a client's communication style
- Generate personalised financial stories
- Provide real-time narrative adaptations based on client responses

Virtual and augmented reality technologies promise immersive storytelling experiences. A client could literally walk through a visual representation of their financial journey, experiencing potential futures and challenges in an interactive, engaging format.

Psychological Resilience Through Narrative

Stories are more than information—they are psychological scaffolding. A well-crafted financial narrative can:

- Transform fear into understanding
- Convert uncertainty into strategic thinking
- Replace anxiety with actionable hope

The most powerful stories don't promise perfect outcomes. They demonstrate human capacity for adaptation, learning, and growth. They show that financial challenges are not insurmountable obstacles, but opportunities for personal transformation.

Practical Storytelling Development

Becoming an exceptional financial storyteller requires deliberate practice:

- Keep a narrative journal of client interactions
- Study successful storytellers across various disciplines
- Practice converting technical concepts into compelling narratives
- Seek feedback on your storytelling approach
- Continuously refine your narrative techniques

Remember, every great financial story has a fundamental structure:

- Relatable Context
- Emotional Resonance
- Strategic Insight
- Transformative Potential

The journey of financial storytelling is ongoing. Each story is an opportunity to connect, to illuminate, to transform understanding.

As you can see, stories have the power to connect, clarify, and inspire. By weaving data and strategy into narratives, you help clients navigate the complexities of financial decisions with greater confidence and ease. But compelling storytelling isn't just about having a strong message; it's about bringing that message to life through relatable characters and real-world scenarios. In the next chapter, we'll delve into the art of crafting characters and narratives that resonate deeply, helping clients see their own journey within the stories you tell.

FIVE KEY TAKEAWAYS

1. Our brains are neurologically wired for stories, activating multiple regions including those responsible for emotions, sensory experiences and decision-making, making financial concepts more memorable than raw data alone.

2. Stories bridge the gap between data and emotion, helping clients not only understand financial concepts intellectually but connect with them emotionally, leading to better retention and action.

3. Financial storytelling has deep historical roots, from ancient fables like "The Ant and the Grasshopper" to modern investment narratives, demonstrating its timeless effectiveness for conveying financial wisdom.

4. Effective financial stories help clients recognise that past performance doesn't guarantee future results, illustrated through analogies like the Christmas turkey who experiences everything going well until it suddenly doesn't.

5. Interactive storytelling creates dialogue rather than monologue, inviting clients to participate in the narrative

CHAPTER 3

Crafting Compelling Narratives

---◆---

"Good storytelling is worth a thousand statistics."
—*Mike LeGassick*

Understanding the power of stories is only the beginning. The next step is to craft narratives that capture your clients' attention and hold it, delivering insights in a way that truly resonates. Compelling narratives don't happen by accident; they require careful thought, a clear purpose, and the right structure. As a financial adviser, every story you tell should have a defined message, rooted in the principles of good planning and investing. This chapter delves into the techniques and strategies to craft narratives that engage, inform, and inspire action.

Defining Your Core Message: What Do You Want to Convey?

Every narrative you craft must have a clear, core message. When you sit down with a client, what is the one thing you want them to walk away with? Start there. This is especially important in financial advising, where clarity is essential.

Think of it like packing for a trip; you wouldn't throw everything into a suitcase; you'd focus on the essentials. This focus is especially important in financial advising, where clarity is key.

To clarify your core message:

1. Brainstorm the key takeaways you want clients to remember from your conversations.
2. Consider the most common pain points, questions, and goals your clients have.
3. Distil these insights into a single, memorable statement that encapsulates your advice.

Examples of core messages include:

- "Diversification spreads risk and builds resilience."
- "Patience and consistency are the keys to investment success."

These statements provide a foundation on which to build your narrative, ensuring it remains meaningful and directed.

The Building Blocks of Effective Storytelling

To tell impactful stories, focus on three key elements:

1. **Relatable Characters:** The characters in your stories should reflect the experiences and aspirations of your clients. To create relatable characters:

- Base them on composite client profiles, incorporating common challenges and goals.
- Use specific details to make them feel authentic, such as their profession, family situation, or hobbies.
- Give them names and personalities that clients can identify with.

2. **A Clear Narrative Arc:** Every story needs a beginning, middle, and end.
   - Beginning: Introduce the character and their financial challenge or goal.
   - Middle: Describe the strategies or actions the character takes to address the challenge.
   - End: Conclude with the outcome and the lessons learnt.

3. **Concrete Imagery**: Use vivid descriptions and analogies to make abstract concepts tangible. For example:
   - Describe market volatility as a roller coaster ride, with ups and downs but an overall upward trajectory.
   - Compare building a diversified portfolio to planting a variety of crops in a field to spread risk.

Understanding Your Audience: Tailoring Stories to Client Needs

Not all stories resonate with every client. Just as each client has unique financial goals, they also differ in their financial knowledge, risk tolerance, and life stages. Tailoring your stories to align with a client's specific experiences, concerns, and aspirations makes your message more relatable.

To gather information about your client's background, goals, and values:

1. Practise active listening during conversations, paying attention to their unique challenges and aspirations.
2. Ask targeted questions about their financial history, current situation, and long-term objectives.
3. Observe their reactions to different scenarios and examples to gauge their risk tolerance and preferences.

Think about each client's background, goals, and values to ensure your story feels personally relevant and engaging. For example:

- For a younger client starting out, a story about building a small savings habit may resonate.
- For a client nearing retirement, a narrative about managing risk while preserving wealth might be more relevant.

Building a Narrative Structure: Beginning, Middle, and End

A well-structured story has a clear beginning, middle, and end. In financial advising, this structure might follow a typical journey:

1. **Beginning:** Introduce a challenge your client faces, such as uncertainty about retirement or fear of market volatility.
2. **Middle:** Outline the strategies or actions taken to address this challenge, using relatable analogies or real-world examples.
3. **End:** Conclude with the outcome or lesson, reinforcing your core message in a way that feels achievable and empowering for your client.

Let's walk through an example of structuring a financial narrative:

Beginning: Introduce Sarah, a 35-year-old entrepreneur who wants to start saving for retirement but fears market volatility.

Middle: Describe how Sarah's adviser recommends a diversified portfolio and a consistent investment strategy. Use the analogy of a balanced diet to illustrate the importance of diversification. Emphasise how regular contributions, like exercise, build financial health over time.

End: Show how Sarah's disciplined approach allows her to weather market ups and downs and build substantial retirement savings. Reinforce the core message that patience and consistency are the keys to long-term success.

The Art of Using Analogies to Simplify Complex Concepts

Analogies are a financial adviser's best friend. They take complex concepts and make them accessible by linking them to something familiar. For example, explaining diversification might feel daunting, but likening it to a balanced diet allows clients to grasp the importance of variety and balance in their portfolio. Similarly, describing compounding interest as the "snowball effect" helps clients visualise how value accumulates over time.

Here are some effective analogies for common concepts:

- **Diversification**: Like not putting all your eggs in one basket.
- **Compound Interest**: Like a snowball growing as it rolls downhill.
- **Asset Allocation**: Like the ingredients in a recipe, each serving a specific purpose.

To craft original analogies:

1. Identify the key characteristics of the financial concept.
2. Brainstorm everyday situations that share those characteristics.
3. Test the analogy with colleagues or friends to ensure it's clear and relatable.

Choose analogies that fit naturally with your clients' everyday experiences. Analogies related to gardening, cooking, or travel, for instance, can resonate widely. The goal is to simplify without oversimplifying, allowing clients to understand the concept's essence while still recognising its importance.

The Subconscious Power of Narrative Bias

People don't just hear stories; they filter them through their existing beliefs. Understanding these subconscious biases allows financial advisers to frame stories in a way that resonates without misleading clients.

Why Clients Believe Some Stories Over Others

People gravitate towards stories that confirm their existing beliefs (confirmation bias). If a client already fears market volatility, they will likely find stories of financial loss more credible than stories about long-term market recovery.

The 'Hero vs. Victim' Narrative Trap Clients interpret financial lessons differently depending on whether a character is portrayed as a hero (e.g., someone who took action and succeeded) or a victim (e.g., someone who suffered a loss due to inaction).

Examples:

- If a story frames a disciplined investor as a hero, risk-averse clients may feel inspired.
- If the same story frames a reckless investor as a victim, it may reinforce fear-driven financial decisions.

Many investors become overly comfortable when markets are performing well, assuming that the good times will last forever. They place increasing amounts of faith in trends, often unaware of the underlying risks. However, just because something has been successful in the past does not mean it will continue indefinitely.

To navigate these biases:

1. Be aware of your own biases and how they may shape your storytelling.
2. Present balanced stories that acknowledge risks but emphasise the potential for long-term success.
3. Frame characters as relatable figures who learn and grow from their experiences.

Creating Emotional Connection Through Personal Stories

Sharing your own experiences can make your narratives more compelling and build trust with clients. Consider sharing stories about:

- An early investment mistake you made and what you learnt from it.
- How you navigated a challenging market environment as a new adviser.

- A client success story that illustrates the power of disciplined investing (anonymised).

When sharing personal stories:

1. Ensure they are relevant to the client's situation and reinforce your core message.
2. Be vulnerable and authentic but maintain professional boundaries.
3. Emphasise the lessons learnt and how they can apply to the client's journey.

Incorporating your own experiences demonstrates that you understand clients' concerns and have faced similar challenges. Personal stories humanise your role as an adviser, fostering a genuine connection.

Practical Applications of Storytelling: Explaining Volatility

Instead of saying, "The stock market can be volatile but tends to trend upwards over time," try this:

"Imagine you're climbing a mountain. There are dips and rises along the trail, but with each step, you're moving closer to the summit. The market works in much the same way. It's not a straight line, but the trajectory over time is upward." Or Imagine you're riding up an escalator while holding a yo-yo in your hand. As you bounce the yo-yo, it drops down and flies back up repeatedly. If you focus solely on the yo-yo, it might seem chaotic—constantly rising and falling. But if you step back and take in the bigger picture, you'll notice something important: the escalator is still moving upward.

This is a perfect analogy for how investments work. The yo-yo represents short-term market movements—the daily ups and downs that many investors obsess over. The escalator, however, represents long-term wealth.

The mistake many investors make is fixating on every dip, every swing, and every alarming headline. When markets drop, they panic and sell everything, waiting for stability before attempting to time their re-entry. When markets move sideways, which can last for years, frustration sets in. They start doubting their strategy, chasing whatever seems to be performing well at the moment—only to discover that what's "hot" today often goes cold tomorrow. In the end, they repeatedly buy high and sell low, a pattern that leads to underperformance. This is why the majority of investors fail to beat the market.

So how do you break free from this emotional trap? The key is to shift your mindset. Most people view investing as a series of short-term speculative bets. But the real investment isn't in the market—it's in you. It's about securing your future, achieving your goals, and ultimately, creating the life you truly want.

Illustrating the Importance of Diversification

Rather than stating, "Diversification reduces risk," say:

"Think of your investments as a fruit basket. If you only have apples and a frost wipes out the apple crop, you've lost everything. But if you have apples, oranges, bananas, and pears, one bad season won't ruin the entire basket."

Practical Example: Crafting a Story About Long-Term Investment

Instead of focusing on market performance charts, share a story like:

"Picture a farmer who plants an orchard. In the early years, there's little to show for the effort — the trees are young, and the yield is small. But the farmer understands that each season of nurturing brings a bigger, healthier harvest. Eventually, the orchard matures, yielding abundant fruit year after year. Investing is similar. The early years might not seem impressive, but with time and patience, the rewards are substantial."

This analogy helps clients view long-term investing as a natural, gradual process, reassuring them that, like nurturing an orchard, their patience will eventually be rewarded, fostering confidence in their financial plan.

Additional examples of applying storytelling to various financial concepts:

- Retirement Planning: "Imagine you're planning a cross-country road trip. Just as you'd map out your route, budget for petrol, and plan your stops, we'll create a roadmap for your retirement journey."
- Risk Management: "Think of insurance like a seatbelt. You hope you never need it, but if an unexpected accident occurs, it can protect you and your loved ones from serious harm."
- Estate Planning: "Consider your estate plan as a love letter to your family. It ensures that your wishes are carried out and that your loved ones are cared for, even after you're gone."

Storytelling Toolkit

To help you craft effective financial narratives, here are some practical tools:

1. Story Starters: Begin with a compelling opening line that introduces the character and their challenge. For example, "When Maria first walked into my office, she had a clear goal in mind but no idea how to get there."
2. Character Development Worksheet: Create a template that outlines key characteristics to consider when developing relatable characters, such as their age, profession, family situation, financial goals, and fears.
3. Analogy Matching Guide: Create a reference guide that matches common financial concepts with relatable analogies. For example:

Case Study: Storytelling in Action

Sarah, a financial adviser, used storytelling to reassure her client, John, who was considering pulling out of the market after a downturn. By sharing relatable stories and analogies, she helped him see why remaining invested during volatility is crucial for long-term success.

Client Situation: John, a 50-year-old sales manager, was considering pulling his investments out of the market after a sharp downturn. He feared losing more money and wasn't sure if he could afford to take the risk.

Story: Sarah shared a story about another client, Mark (anonymised), who had faced a similar situation during the 2008 financial crisis. Despite Sarah's advice to stay invested, Mark panicked and sold his portfolio at a loss. In the years that followed, Mark missed out on the market recovery and had to delay his retirement.

Sarah then shared a personal story about how she had felt the same fear during past market crashes but had learnt to trust in the long-term growth potential of a diversified portfolio. She used the analogy of a tree weathering a storm—bending but not breaking and growing stronger over time.

Outcome: John realised that selling now would only lock in his losses and jeopardise his long-term goals. He decided to stay invested and focus on the long-term growth potential of his portfolio.

Her personal story built trust and credibility, while the analogy made the abstract concept of market resilience more tangible.

Empowering Clients Through Compelling Narratives

Crafting compelling narratives is more than an art; it's a skill that can significantly enhance your effectiveness as an adviser. When done well, storytelling empowers clients to make informed decisions, deepens their understanding, and builds a sense of trust. By focusing on your core message, tailoring stories to each client, and using relatable analogies, you can transform complex financial concepts into insights that clients feel equipped to act on.

Remember, effective financial storytelling involves:

1. Defining a clear, core message
2. Creating relatable characters and a clear narrative arc
3. Using concrete imagery and analogies to simplify complex concepts
4. Tailoring stories to each client's unique needs and goals
5. Navigating narrative biases by presenting balanced, growth-oriented stories

6. Building emotional connection through vulnerable, relevant personal stories
7. Continuously practising and refining your storytelling skills

By mastering the art of storytelling, you can empower your clients to make informed decisions, deepen their understanding, and feel confident in their financial journey. In the next chapter, we'll explore how to create characters and personas that make these stories even more relatable, helping clients see themselves in the narratives you craft.

FIVE KEY TAKEAWAYS

1. Every narrative must have a clear, core message that serves as the foundation—like "Diversification spreads risk and builds resilience" or "Patience and consistency are the keys to investment success."

2. Effective financial stories require three key elements: relatable characters that reflect clients' experiences, a clear narrative arc (beginning, middle, and end), and concrete imagery that makes abstract concepts tangible.

3. Analogies are powerful tools for simplifying complex financial concepts, such as comparing diversification to not putting all eggs in one basket or compound interest to a snowball growing as it rolls downhill.

4. Tailoring stories to align with each client's specific experiences, concerns, and life stage makes your message more personally relevant and engaging, resulting in better understanding and retention.

5. Personal stories and experiences create emotional connections with clients, demonstrating that you understand their concerns because you've faced similar challenges, which helps build trust and credibility.

CHAPTER 4

Creating Relatable Characters

---◇---

"A story is only as strong as its characters. Give them depth, make them relatable, and they'll carry the message for you."
—*Neil Gaiman*

Characters are the heart of any story, and in financial storytelling, they provide clients with a relatable lens through which to view complex financial concepts. A well-crafted character can bridge the gap between abstract ideas and real-life application, making financial advice more accessible and impactful. In this chapter, we'll explore how to create relatable client personas, use real-life examples, and craft characters that clients can see themselves in.

Using Client Personas to Build Stories

In financial storytelling, your characters don't need to be fictional. Often, they represent the typical clients you work with, facing common challenges such as planning for retirement, saving for a child's education, or managing investment risk. By developing detailed personas, you can create stories that resonate with your clients' unique backgrounds, goals, and financial circumstances.

A client persona is essentially a fictional profile based on real client characteristics, embodying the traits, motivations, and challenges of your target audience. For example, you might have personas like:

- "Sophie," a 35-year-old professional looking to build a financial safety net while planning for her family's future.
- "James," a 60-year-old business owner who is preparing for retirement but is unsure how to transition his assets smoothly.

Beyond Basic Demographics: A Comprehensive Persona Framework

While traditional persona development focuses on surface-level characteristics, truly effective financial storytelling requires a multi-dimensional approach.

Psychological Profiling

Develop a deeper understanding of your clients by exploring:

- Financial personality types
- Individual risk tolerance
- Emotional relationship with money
- Unique decision-making patterns

Client Archetype Insights

Recognise the distinct personas that emerge in financial planning:

1. **The Cautious Planner**
   - Seeks financial security above all else

- Requires detailed, methodical strategic planning
- Responds best to conservative, step-by-step narratives

2. **The Ambitious Achiever**
- Driven by growth and potential
- Eager for innovative investment strategies
- Inspired by stories of strategic financial breakthroughs

3. **The Emotional Investor**
- Decisions deeply influenced by personal experiences
- Needs empathetic, narrative-driven guidance
- Connects through stories of financial transformation

Generational and Cultural Considerations

When building personas, consider:

- Unique financial perspectives across different generations
- Cultural influences on financial decision-making
- Diverse backgrounds and life experiences

When building client personas, continue to include traditional elements:

- **Demographics:** Age, career stage, family situation, and income level.
- **Financial Goals:** Short-term and long-term objectives, such as buying a home, planning for retirement, or preserving wealth.
- **Challenges and Fears:** Common financial worries like market volatility, inflation, or running out of money in retirement.
- **Values and Priorities:** Personal values, such as leaving a legacy, maintaining financial independence, or supporting loved ones.

These elements help you create a character that feels authentic, ensuring your clients can see themselves or someone they know in the story. Using personas in storytelling isn't about oversimplifying or stereotyping but rather creating a framework that allows your advice to feel relevant and grounded in clients' realities.

Real-Life Examples: Bringing the Abstract to Life

Incorporating real-life examples into your storytelling adds authenticity and credibility. Sharing anonymised case studies, success stories, or common scenarios from your own practice can demonstrate the tangible benefits of your advice and make complex financial ideas more relatable.

Ethical Storytelling Considerations

To maintain integrity while sharing powerful narratives:

Anonymisation Techniques

- Create composite characters by blending multiple client experiences
- Always obtain explicit consent for story sharing
- Remove specific identifiable details while preserving narrative essence

Psychological Safety

- Ensure stories empower rather than expose vulnerabilities
- Focus on growth and positive transformation
- Respect the emotional complexity of financial journeys

When using real-life examples, consider:

1. **Anonymity and Confidentiality:** Ensure client privacy by anonymising details and focusing on the general principles rather than specific personal information.

2. **Highlighting Challenges and Solutions:** Describe the client's initial concerns, the strategies you implemented, and the positive outcomes achieved. For example, if you're explaining the importance of diversification, you might share a story of a client who avoided major losses during a market dip by having a well-balanced portfolio.
3. **Making Success Attainable:** Use examples that show achievable steps clients can take, avoiding stories that may feel out of reach or overly complex.

A story about a couple in their 40s balancing retirement savings with education costs for their children could resonate with clients in a similar life stage, helping them see that they're not alone in facing these challenges. By weaving real-life examples into your narratives, you help clients envision their own path to financial success, making the abstract concepts more tangible and motivating.

Crafting Characters Clients Can See Themselves In

Relatable characters are those that clients can identify with, seeing their own lives reflected in the story. This makes the advice feel more relevant and actionable. Crafting characters that clients can empathise with requires attention to the finer details of their lives, motivations, and challenges.

Psychological Dimensions of Financial Storytelling: Narrative Transportation Theory

Financial narratives have the power to:

- Allow clients to mentally simulate financial scenarios
- Influence behavioural change
- Create deeper emotional engagement with financial concepts

Cognitive Empathy in Financial Communication

Develop stories that:

- Demonstrate genuine understanding of client challenges
- Use emotional intelligence to craft relatable narratives
- Bridge the gap between professional advice and personal experience

To create characters clients can connect with, consider:

- **Reflecting Common Client Concerns:** Address issues your clients are likely facing, such as retirement anxiety, uncertainty about investment choices, or balancing short-term needs with long-term goals.
    - For instance, a character like "Emma," a 45-year-old working mother anxious about saving enough for retirement and her children's future, reflects the concerns of many clients balancing competing priorities.
- **Using Everyday Language:** Craft characters who speak and think in ways clients can relate to. Avoid heavy financial jargon; instead, create characters who ask straightforward questions, express doubts, or seek clarity. This helps clients feel understood and shows that financial advising is approachable, not intimidating.
- **Making Characters Proactive and Empowered:** Design characters who, through guidance, take an active role in their financial journey. Instead of depicting characters as passive recipients of advice, show them making decisions, overcoming setbacks, and achieving their goals with your help. For example, a story might follow "Tom," a small business owner, who, with your guidance, creates a retirement plan that provides him with confidence for the future.

- **Acknowledging Real Struggles and Triumphs:** Share stories that involve both challenges and successes. For instance, a character who initially makes impulsive financial decisions due to market anxieties but gradually learns to stay calm and committed to their plan demonstrates both vulnerability and growth, making them more relatable.

By crafting characters who embody real client concerns and emotions, you make your advice feel personal and attainable. Clients are more likely to engage with a character's story when they see parallels to their own lives, allowing your guidance to resonate on a deeper level.

Navigating the Complexity of Financial Narratives

Financial stories are never as straightforward as we might imagine. They are intricate journeys that defy simple categorisation, weaving together threads of personal history, emotional landscape, and nuanced decision-making that extend far beyond traditional storytelling frameworks.

Consider for a moment the true nature of a financial journey. It is not a linear path with clear signposts, but a complex ecosystem of interconnected experiences. Each financial decision is like a stone dropped into a pond, creating ripples that extend far beyond the initial moment of choice. A decision to invest, to save, or to take a financial risk is never just about numbers—it is about hopes, fears, family histories, and deeply personal aspirations.

The most compelling financial narratives emerge when we acknowledge this complexity. They reject the simplistic notion of a hero's triumphant march or a victim's tragic defeat. Instead, they embrace the beautiful messiness of human experience—the moments of uncertainty, the unexpected turns, the subtle interplay between rational thinking and emotional intuition.

Take, for example, the story of Maria, a professional who inherited a complex relationship with money from her family. Her financial journey isn't a neat progression from struggle to success, but a nuanced exploration of self-discovery. Her decisions are shaped by layers of experience: her parents' cautious approach to finances, her own professional ambitions, the cultural expectations that surround her, and the deeply personal fears and hopes that whisper beneath the surface of each financial choice.

Financial advisers who truly understand their clients recognise that every financial story is a multidimensional narrative. It is simultaneously about professional goals and personal dreams, about risk management and emotional security, about immediate needs and long-term aspirations. These stories cannot be confined to simple templates or predictable arcs.

The most powerful approach is to view financial narratives as living, breathing ecosystems. They are not static documents to be filed away, but dynamic conversations between possibility and preparedness. Each client brings a unique constellation of experiences—generational patterns, cultural influences, personal traumas, and unexpected moments of inspiration—that shape their financial worldview.

This complexity demands a radical reimagining of how we tell financial stories. It requires us to move beyond linear thinking, to embrace uncertainty as a fundamental aspect of financial planning. The most effective financial advisers are those who can navigate this complexity with empathy, insight, and a profound respect for the individual's unique journey.

Imagine financial storytelling as a form of cartography, where we are not drawing fixed maps but creating adaptable navigational tools. We are not predicting the future but preparing for its inherent uncertainty. We are helping clients develop a kind of financial resilience that goes beyond mere numbers—a resilience rooted in self-understanding, emotional intelligence, and the capacity to adapt.

The true art of financial storytelling lies in this delicate balance: providing structure and guidance while simultaneously honouring the unpredictable, deeply personal nature of each individual's financial journey. It is about creating narratives that are at once grounded and expansive, practical, and inspirational.

As financial advisers, our role is not to simplify or reduce these complex stories, but to illuminate their nuanced beauty. We are translators, helping clients understand the rich, multifaceted language of their own financial potential.

This emotional complexity often shows itself most clearly during times of uncertainty. Even the best-laid financial plans can be derailed when fear creeps in, prompting clients to react in ways that feel protective but are ultimately harmful. A vivid illustration of this comes from a story I often share with clients.

Rearranging Deckchairs

One of the most absurd — and yet strangely human — images from history is this: the Titanic is sinking. The ship is listing dangerously. Panic is spreading. And on the top deck, a sharply dressed gentleman is calmly rearranging the deckchairs.

It sounds ridiculous, doesn't it? But it's exactly what many investors (and even some advisers) do when markets wobble.

The Titanic didn't sink because of a storm everyone could see gathering on the horizon. It sank because of an unseen iceberg — a hidden danger no one fully anticipated. And that's a crucial lesson: it's not always the obvious threats we prepare for that hurt us most. It's the ones we don't see coming. No one practises lifeboat drills after the iceberg hits. By then, it's too late. Preparation has to happen before the crisis, not during it — just as smart financial planning prepares clients to weather the unknown, not react to it.

When the market suddenly drops, fear kicks in. And instead of trusting their long-term plan, many investors start rearranging —

tweaking portfolios by 1%, switching funds, nervously dialling down equities. It feels like action. It feels like protection. But in reality, it's often just movement — not improvement.

This is the illusion of control. When uncertainty strikes, doing something — anything — makes us feel better. But when you've built a solid, evidence-based, long-term plan, fiddling around isn't just unnecessary. It can actually make things worse.

I often remind clients: "We didn't build your plan to sail only when the skies are clear. We built it strong enough to survive the unknowns we can't predict."

Changing your portfolio mid-storm — or mid-iceberg — isn't about logic. It's about emotion.

And that's where real advice matters most: helping clients trust their plan through the noise, the fear, and the unexpected events.

So next time the markets wobble, the headlines scream, and the instinct to "tinker just a little" creeps in, ask yourself: "Am I truly improving the plan — or just rearranging deckchairs?"

Because in the end, the real value isn't found in moving chairs. It's found in building ships strong enough to sail through whatever comes — even the things we can't see coming.

Practical Example: Developing a Story for a Young Investor

Imagine you're advising a young client, "Sarah," who is just starting to save for her future but feels overwhelmed by the idea of investing. Instead of overwhelming her with technical information, you might frame her story as a simple, relatable journey:

"Sarah, like many young professionals, has a busy life and often thinks she has plenty of time to start investing. But with guidance, she begins setting aside a small portion of her monthly income. At first, the growth is slow, but over the years, her small contributions start to grow, like seeds planted in a garden. The plants don't appear overnight, but with regular care, they bloom beautifully in time."

This story helps young clients like Sarah understand that even modest investments can grow significantly over time. By making Sarah's story relatable and achievable, you encourage clients to take proactive steps toward their own financial goals.

Building Connection Through Relatable Characters

Relatable characters breathe life into financial advice, transforming abstract concepts into stories that clients can see themselves in. By using client personas, sharing anonymised real-life examples, and crafting characters that reflect common client concerns, you create narratives that are engaging, informative, and ultimately empowering.

Continuous Persona Refinement

Treat client personas as living documents:

- Conduct regular reviews and updates
- Incorporate feedback from changing client demographics
- Adapt to evolving financial landscapes
- Maintain a flexible, responsive approach to client representation

In crafting these characters, you guide clients through their financial journeys in a way that feels personal, relevant, and achievable. In the next chapter, we'll explore how to set the scene and provide context, making your stories even more immersive and impactful by grounding them in real-world scenarios and familiar environments. This next step helps reinforce your clients' understanding, ensuring your stories resonate long after they leave your office.

SIX KEY TAKEAWAYS

1. Characters provide clients with a relatable lens through which to view complex financial concepts, bridging the gap between abstract ideas and real-life application.
2. Creating comprehensive client personas goes beyond basic demographics to include psychological profiles, financial personality types, and cultural considerations that reflect your clients' unique backgrounds.
3. Anonymised real-life examples add authenticity and credibility to your stories while maintaining client confidentiality through composite characters and removed identifiable details.
4. The most powerful financial narratives embrace complexity, acknowledging that financial decisions are influenced by hopes, fears, family histories, and personal aspirations rather than just numbers.
5. Crafting characters who express common concerns in everyday language, demonstrate both vulnerability and growth, and take an active role in their financial journey helps clients see themselves in the story.
6. Emotional resilience is vital in financial storytelling. By helping clients understand that preparation, not reaction, is the key to navigating uncertainty, advisers build stronger, more confident decision-makers who are better equipped to weather unexpected events.

CHAPTER 5

Setting the Scene: Context is King

"Without context, words and actions have no meaning at all."
—*Gregory Bateson*

In the intricate landscape of financial communication, context is the master storyteller—a subtle yet powerful force that transforms abstract numerical concepts into living, breathing narratives of human aspiration and possibility. Financial advisers are not merely number crunchers, but story architects who construct bridges of understanding between complex financial realities and individual human experiences.

Never forget that context is everything. When explaining complex financial concepts, context serves as the foundation for your story. It provides clients with a framework to understand the relevance of your advice, making abstract ideas feel grounded and real. Imagine watching a movie where a scene suddenly shifts to a stormy sea without warning—without the build-up of dark clouds or ominous music, the tension is lost, and the scene feels disconnected. In the same way, offering financial advice without setting the scene leaves clients without the perspective needed to appreciate its value.

The human mind is fundamentally a narrative processing machine. We make sense of the world through stories, filtering complex information through the lens of personal and collective experiences. Financial decisions are never mere mathematical calculations, but profound emotional journeys that intersect with the most intimate aspects of human experience. Each financial choice carries the weight of personal history, familial expectations, cultural conditioning, and individual hopes.

To truly engage clients, begin each story with a contextual backdrop that aligns with current events, economic trends, or individual client concerns. Whether it's addressing the impact of rising inflation, discussing shifting pension regulations, or highlighting recent changes in tax laws, grounding your story in the real world makes your advice feel timely and impactful. Setting the scene brings your message into focus, helping clients see its direct relevance to their lives and decisions.

Effective financial storytelling requires more than technical expertise. It demands a profound empathy that allows advisers to see beyond spreadsheets and investment charts, recognising the human narrative that gives those numbers their true meaning. Context is the lens that transforms financial advice from a transactional interaction into a meaningful dialogue about possibility, security, and personal potential.

The Contextual Landscape

Context is not a static backdrop, but a dynamic, living ecosystem. It shifts with personal circumstances, economic changes, and individual growth. An effective financial narrative must be equally adaptable, capable of evolving alongside the client's journey. This requires financial advisers to become true narrative archaeologists—carefully excavating the layers of experience that inform a client's financial worldview.

Every client arrives with a unique story—a complex tapestry woven from personal histories, cultural influences, and individual aspirations. The most compelling financial stories emerge when advisers recognise this complexity, moving beyond one-size-fits-all approaches to create truly personalised narratives of financial possibility.

Using Real-World Events to Ground Your Stories

Real-world events are the narrative anchors of financial storytelling—powerful contextual markers that transform abstract concepts into tangible, relatable experiences. They provide clients with a familiar landscape through which complex financial ideas can be explored, understood, and internalised.

Real-world events provide an anchor that clients can relate to, making your advice more accessible and believable. By referencing events in the news, economic shifts, or changes in regulations, you give clients a context that makes complex financial concepts more understandable.

The Anatomy of Contextual Storytelling

Every significant economic event carries within it a multitude of human stories. A market fluctuation is never just a numerical change, but a complex narrative of human hopes, fears, collective behaviour, and individual decision-making. When financial advisers learn to read these events as rich, multilayered narratives, they transform from mere analysts to true storytellers.

For example, if inflation is rising, you might start your story by discussing how increased prices impact everyday purchases, from groceries to travel. Then, you can segue into how inflation affects long-term savings or retirement plans. By doing so, you help clients connect personal financial choices to broader economic forces, illustrating the importance of adjusting their financial strategies in response to real-world changes.

The Silent Economic Predator: Understanding Inflation

Inflation is far more than a sterile economic statistic. It is a relentless economic force that quietly erodes wealth, transforming financial dreams into increasingly distant mirages. Like a slow-moving predator, inflation gradually consumes purchasing power, making everything from daily necessities to lifelong goals progressively more expensive.

But inflation is not just a number on a chart, or an abstract concept discussed by economists. It is a relentless force, one that quietly erodes wealth over time, making everything from daily necessities to lifelong goals more expensive. While clients might feel its effects when grocery bills increase or travel becomes more costly, inflation's true danger lies in its slow and persistent nature, gradually weakening the purchasing power of their savings.

In popular culture, we often see figures that are relentless, unstoppable, and immune to reason. Take, for instance, the iconic terminator from James Cameron's 1984 science fiction film. Much like the original Terminator who was an unstoppable machine, inflation, when unleashed, can be an equally unyielding force in the realm of economics. As a playful allusion to the movie, consider this: "Listen and understand. That inflation is out there. It can't be bargained with. It can't be reasoned with. It doesn't feel pity, or remorse, or fear and it absolutely will not stop, ever, until your purchasing power is dead." This analogy might sound dramatic, but it vividly illustrates to the listener that the dangers and persistent nature of uncontrolled inflation cannot be understated.

A Metaphorical Journey Through Economic Challenges

In the world of finance, there are obvious threats and then there are silent ones. Like a boa constrictor wrapping itself around its prey, inflation might not deliver an immediate lethal squeeze, but its effects are undeniable over time. The prey, in this case, are our dreams, aspirations, and the legacy we intend to leave behind.

The psychological impact of inflation extends far beyond mere numbers. It touches the very core of human financial security, creating a persistent undercurrent of anxiety. Clients might feel its effects when grocery bills unexpectedly surge or travel becomes prohibitively expensive, but inflation's true danger lies in its insidious, gradual nature.

Cultural and Generational Perspectives

Different generations and cultural backgrounds interpret economic challenges through unique lenses. A client who experienced economic hardship during a previous recession will approach financial planning with a fundamentally different perspective compared to someone who has only known periods of economic stability. These varied experiences create rich, nuanced narratives that demand careful, empathetic understanding.

When using real-world events, consider these critical dimensions:

1. **Relevance:** Choose events that resonate deeply with your client's specific life circumstances. For a young professional, trends in the job market or changes in student loan policies might be far more impactful than abstract discussions of retirement planning.

2. **Clarity:** Navigate the delicate balance between providing sufficient context and avoiding overwhelming technical details. Your goal is to illuminate, not to confuse.
3. **Insight:** Move beyond surface-level event reporting. Help clients understand how these broader economic shifts might directly impact their personal financial journey and decision-making.

By grounding your stories in real-world events, you do more than provide information. You create a bridge of understanding that helps clients feel more prepared, more confident, and more empowered to navigate their financial futures.

Why Investors React the Way They Do - And How to Make These Lessons Stick Through Storytelling

The human mind is a labyrinth of complex psychological mechanisms, nowhere more evident than in the realm of financial decision-making. Investors are not the rational, calculating machines of economic theory, but intricate beings driven by a profound interplay of emotions, learned experiences, and deeply ingrained psychological patterns.

Understanding how human psychology influences investment decisions is crucial to making smarter financial choices. People like to believe they are rational decision-makers, but in reality, emotions, habits, and subconscious biases often shape their actions. These biases don't just affect individual investment decisions—they also influence how people react to news headlines, market fluctuations, and economic changes.

The Psychological Landscape of Financial Decision-Making

At the heart of financial psychology lies a fundamental truth: our brains are not designed for modern financial complexity. They are evolutionary machines shaped by millennia of survival instincts that often work against sophisticated financial planning. The same mechanisms that once helped our ancestors survive in unpredictable environments now create sophisticated psychological traps in the world of investing.

Even the most intelligent and experienced investors are not immune to these mental mechanisms. The way we process information, respond to risk, and make decisions is often influenced by hidden psychological forces that operate just beneath the surface of conscious awareness.

Some of these tendencies are rooted in our most fundamental survival instincts. Others emerge from the brain's remarkable ability to simplify complex information. Whether it's fearing losses more than valuing gains, following the crowd instead of thinking independently, or placing too much weight on recent events, these psychological patterns can quietly steer investors in destructive directions.

The Power of Storytelling in Psychological Insight

This is where storytelling becomes a powerful tool. By framing these biases in relatable, everyday scenarios, investors can recognise them in their own behaviour and make better decisions. A well-told story makes abstract psychological concepts feel real, allowing people to see themselves in the narrative rather than simply reading dry financial theory.

The most compelling approach to understanding investor behaviour is not through theoretical analysis, but through stories that illuminate the complex psychological landscape of financial decision-making. Stories create a bridge of understanding, allowing clients to see their own psychological patterns from a new, more objective perspective.

Exploring Psychological Biases Through Narrative

In the realm of investing, recency bias can be particularly destructive. When markets have been rising, investors may become irrationally exuberant, assuming the upward trajectory will continue indefinitely. Conversely, during a market downturn, the same mechanism can trigger profound pessimism, leading investors to assume further declines are inevitable.

The psychological roots of these biases are not weaknesses to be ashamed of, but natural human mechanisms to be understood and navigated. By recognising these patterns, investors can develop more thoughtful, measured approaches to financial decision-making.

Financial advisers who master this psychological terrain become more than technical experts. They become trusted guides, helping clients understand the complex inner workings of their own financial decision-making processes.

Psychological Biases: Navigating the Hidden Forces of Financial Decision-Making

The human mind is a complex landscape of psychological mechanisms that profoundly influence financial decision-making. Each bias represents a fascinating window into our cognitive processes, revealing the intricate ways our brains attempt to simplify complex information and manage uncertainty so let's take a deeper dive into some of the most common investor biases.

Recency Bias: The Tyranny of Immediate Experience

Imagine a torrential rainstorm that drenches you on your way home from work—a sudden, memorable deluge that seeps into your clothes and memory. The next morning, despite meteorological predictions of bright sunshine, you instinctively grab an umbrella. For days afterwards, you remain hyper-aware of potential rain, your perception skewed by that single recent experience.

This is recency bias—a profound psychological mechanism that reveals the remarkable yet often misleading way our brains process information. Our cognitive systems are evolutionary relics, designed to prioritise immediate, vivid experiences over long-term statistical thinking. What worked as a survival mechanism in our ancestral environments can become a dangerous cognitive trap in modern financial decision-making.

Sir John Templeton, one of the most respected investors of the 20th century, understood this psychological pitfall intimately. His famous warning, "This time it's different," was a powerful reminder of how easily investors can fall prey to the illusion that current market conditions represent a new, permanent reality.

The psychological roots of recency bias lie deep in our evolutionary past. Our brains evolved to prioritise recent, vivid information as a survival mechanism. In primitive environments, paying close attention to recent events could mean the difference between life and death. A recent encounter with a predator, for instance, would demand heightened vigilance. But in the complex world of modern investing, this same mechanism can lead to profoundly irrational decision-making.

Neurologically, recency bias is a testament to the brain's remarkable ability to create shortcuts and heuristics.

Heuristics are mental shortcuts or rules of thumb that humans use to make decisions quickly, especially in complex or uncertain situations.

Our cognitive systems are constantly filtering vast amounts of information, and recent experiences provide convenient, easily accessible data points. The problem arises when we mistake these recent experiences for comprehensive truth, overlooking broader patterns and long-term trends.

- For investors, understanding recency bias is more than an intellectual exercise—it's a critical skill for financial survival. It requires developing a disciplined approach that consciously challenges our brain's natural tendency to overemphasise recent events. This means cultivating:
- A historical perspective that looks beyond immediate experiences
- Statistical thinking that values long-term trends over short-term fluctuations
- Emotional discipline that can resist the seductive pull of recent, vivid experiences

The most successful investors are those who can step back from the immediacy of recent events, recognising them as mere moments in a much larger financial landscape. They understand that market movements are cyclical, that today's seemingly revolutionary trend is tomorrow's forgotten footnote.

Templeton's wisdom continues to resonate: financial markets are complex, dynamic systems that defy simple narratives. "This time it's different" is rarely true—and believing it can be the costliest bias of all.

The Battlefield Perspective: Strategy Over Skirmishes

Building on this cyclical understanding, successful investors adopt what might be called a "battlefield perspective" - recognising that the investment journey isn't about avoiding every setback but about ensuring that your final destination aligns with your objectives, regardless of the inevitably turbulent path to get there.

Markets rise and fall with the predictability of tides, yet with the unpredictability of their magnitude. A 2% drop can trigger panic, while a 3% gain might inspire unwarranted confidence. Both reactions miss the essential truth: these are merely battles in a much longer war.

Consider the investors who maintained their positions and strategy during the 2008 financial crisis. While many surrendered and locked in permanent losses, those who held firm eventually witnessed not just recovery but substantial growth in the following decade. They lost several battles but ultimately won the war.

This approach requires a fundamental perspective shift—from obsessing about what markets will do tomorrow to positioning for what they will achieve over decades:

- The investor worrying about next quarter's earnings report is playing draughts
- The investor positioning for decade-long technological transformation is playing chess
- The investor building wealth across generations is playing a game beyond conventional scorekeeping

This shift isn't merely philosophical—it's practical. Research consistently demonstrates that investors who trade frequently in response to short-term events underperform those who maintain long-term conviction.

Implementing this battlefield perspective requires both strategic planning and psychological discipline:

1. Define ultimate objectives: What are you truly trying to achieve? Financial independence? Educational funding? Generational wealth? The war's objective must be crystal clear.

2. Create appropriate time horizons: Match your investment approach to the actual timeframe of your goals, not to arbitrary market cycles.

3. Develop battle-loss tolerance: Determine in advance how much temporary decline you can withstand without abandoning strategy.
4. Establish victory metrics: Define how you'll measure success based on progress toward ultimate goals, not interim performance.

Perhaps the greatest challenge in this approach is that it requires both continuous conviction and patient restraint—seemingly contradictory qualities. The investor must simultaneously believe deeply in their strategy while resisting the urge to constantly adjust it.

Warren Buffett's famous advice captures this paradox perfectly: "The stock market is a device for transferring money from the impatient to the patient." The impatient lose battles and abandon the war; the patient may lose battles but position themselves to win the ultimate campaign.

The next time market volatility triggers anxiety, remind your clients that they're witnessing one battle in a much longer war. Their ultimate financial success depends not on avoiding every loss, but on ensuring that their overarching strategy aligns with the remarkable power of markets to create wealth over time. When markets wobble, remind your clients that volatility is a skirmish, but strategy is your stronghold.

From Concept to Conversation: Bringing the Battlefield Story to Life

So how do you help clients truly understand this battlefield mindset — and act on it? Here's how to turn metaphor into meaningful dialogue.

Reframe short-term noise

"We're not trying to win every skirmish — we're here to win the campaign."

Use this when clients focus too heavily on short-term moves or financial news.

Remind them of their objective

"The war we're fighting isn't against volatility — it's for your freedom, your security, and your legacy."

This brings emotional clarity back to the conversation.

Reinforce strategic discipline

"We expect to lose a few battles. The goal is not to abandon the strategy when we do."

This helps the client normalise downturns and stay focused.

Embrace the paradox

"Winning the war requires two things that feel at odds — conviction and restraint."

Let the client sit with this. It reframes investing as an emotional discipline as much as a financial one. To bring it all together, invite your client into the future:

"If we look back ten years from now, what would need to have happened for you to say, 'We won the war'?"

Prospect Theory: The Emotional Mathematics of Gain and Loss

Finding a £20 note on the pavement is a pleasant surprise—it feels like a little financial win. But losing £20 from your pocket feels much worse than the joy of finding it. The emotional impact of the loss is far greater than the equivalent gain.

This is prospect theory in action, a psychological phenomenon that unveils the asymmetrical nature of human emotional responses. Our brains are not rational calculators but complex emotional engines that process financial information through a deeply personal lens. The pain of losing money is psychologically more intense than the pleasure of gaining the same amount—a quirk of human psychology that can lead to fundamentally irrational financial behaviours.

In investing, prospect theory manifests in profound ways. Investors often hold onto losing investments too long, hoping they will recover, or sell winning investments too soon just to lock in a small profit. The underlying mechanism is an attempt to avoid the acute psychological pain of loss, even when such actions contradict rational financial strategy.

From Concept to Conversation: Turning Prospect Theory into Client Dialogue

Prospect theory reveals one of the most powerful emotional truths in investing: losses feel worse than gains feel good.

This insight helps explain why rational plans are so often abandoned during emotional moments. Your role as an adviser isn't just to manage portfolios — it's to guide clients through the emotional asymmetry that prospect theory exposes.

Here's how to bring this behavioural insight into your client conversations in a way that resonates:

Reframe the fear of loss

"It's completely normal to feel more upset about losing money than excited about gaining it. That's not weakness — that's wiring."

By normalising the emotional response, you remove the sting of self-judgement. Clients feel understood rather than corrected, which lowers resistance and builds trust.

Translate emotion into structure

"That feeling is exactly why we follow a strategy. It's there to protect you from making a decision that feels right in the moment but could work against your long-term plan."

This allows you to position the financial plan as an emotional stabiliser — not just a numbers exercise.

Gently challenge reactive behaviour

If a client wants to sell a falling investment or lock in a small gain prematurely, you can say:

"What you're experiencing right now is the discomfort prospect theory predicts. The pain of the current drop is louder than the logic of long-term growth."

Then follow with a reflective question:

"If this same investment had gone up instead of down, would you be rushing to sell it — or would you be letting it run?"

This approach doesn't push back forcefully. It invites perspective, helping the client challenge their own thinking without feeling exposed.

Re-centre the conversation on their objective

"Our plan is designed to get you to your long-term goal, not just to make today feel better. We're playing the long game — and short-term discomfort is part of that journey."

This gently pulls the client's focus back to progress over perfection — to movement, not moment.

Prompt future perspective

One of the most effective reframing tools is to move the client forward in time:

"If we were having this conversation a year from now and markets had recovered, how would you feel about the decision you're about to make today?"

It creates emotional distance from the present moment and allows reason to re-enter the conversation.

Prospect theory helps explain why clients often resist good advice — not because they don't understand, but because their emotional response overrides their rational judgement. When you bring awareness to that dynamic, and pair it with calm, long-term framing, you're doing more than just helping them stay invested.

You're helping them grow into the kind of investor who can weather storms without abandoning their ship — and that's where real success happens.

Confirmation Bias: The Comfort of Familiar Narratives

A tea drinker who swears by the health benefits of green tea will happily absorb every article that confirms this belief. But if they come across research suggesting it might not be as beneficial as they thought, they dismiss it as flawed or untrustworthy.

Confirmation bias is a deeply ingrained psychological mechanism that protects our existing worldviews. It's a cognitive shortcut that helps us maintain a sense of certainty in an uncertain world. In financial decision-making, this bias can be particularly dangerous. Investors who believe a particular stock is a great investment will actively seek out information that reinforces their view while systematically ignoring or discounting contradictory evidence.

From Concept to Conversation: Helping Clients See the Full Picture

Confirmation bias is rarely loud or obvious. It shows up in quiet ways — a client repeatedly quoting the same article, dismissing uncomfortable data, or "doing research" that always supports what they already believe. The risk isn't just bad information — it's unbalanced information.

Your role as an adviser is to gently disrupt the comfort of one-sided thinking without making the client feel foolish or defensive. This requires empathy, skill, and carefully chosen questions.

Invite broader reflection

"You might be right — and it's always helpful to ask: what evidence would I need to see before I changed my mind?"

This shifts the focus from defending a belief to testing its strength.

Use both-sides framing

"I've seen research that supports your view — and I've also seen some that challenges it. Can we take a look at both together before we decide?"

This positions you as a collaborative thinker, not a challenger.

Introduce the idea of portfolio balance as a guardrail

"Confirmation bias is exactly why we don't let any one belief drive the whole plan. Diversification protects us — not just from the market, but from ourselves."

This reframes discipline as wisdom, not restriction.

Bring it back to the bigger picture

"We don't need to be right about every detail — we need to be broadly right about the direction we're heading. That's what your plan is designed to do."

Clients often cling to certainty because it feels safer. But when you help them embrace balance over bias, you offer something better than certainty — you offer perspective.

As economist John Maynard Keynes once said:

"When the facts change, I change my mind — what do you do, sir?"

Used well, that quote becomes more than a soundbite. It becomes permission — for the client to adjust, adapt, and grow.

Overreaction Bias: The Emotional Rollercoaster of Market Perception

A football team concedes a goal in the first five minutes of a match. Their supporters immediately panic, assuming they are going to lose. But over the course of the match, they settle down, play well, and eventually win comfortably.

Overreaction bias reveals the profound emotional volatility that underlies human decision-making. In financial markets, this manifests as dramatic, often irrational responses to short-term events. When markets fall sharply, investors may panic-sell, believing the decline will continue indefinitely. This knee-jerk reaction ignores the fundamental reality of market cycles and long-term investment strategies.

From Concept to Conversation: Calming the Emotional Snap Response

Overreaction bias feeds on immediacy. Something happens — a drop in the market, a headline, a dip in portfolio value — and the emotional brain surges forward with urgency: *"Do something now."*

But reacting impulsively to short-term noise often leads to long-term regret. Your job as the adviser is to help the client slow down, zoom out, and reconnect with the broader story — the one they committed to before emotions took the wheel.

Acknowledge the emotion without validating the impulse

"I completely understand why that drop feels unsettling. The urge to act is strong — and totally human."

This disarms defensiveness and opens the door for a more thoughtful conversation.

Use pattern recognition to ground the conversation

"We've seen this before. A sharp drop. A lot of noise. And then, eventually, a recovery. The danger isn't the decline itself — it's making a decision during the emotional spike."

This reframes the situation as a pattern, not a crisis.

Anchor the client back to their personal plan

"Your plan wasn't built for just the good days. It's designed to carry you through exactly this sort of turbulence — with your long-term goal still intact."

This helps them re-centre on structure, not sensation.

Use a future-frame to shift perspective

"If we fast-forward five years and this market drop has fully recovered — how would you feel looking back on a panic decision made today?"

This creates distance between the moment and the consequence, which reduces reactivity.

Introduce the concept of a 'cooling-off lens'

"Whenever the market moves dramatically, we apply a cooling-off lens: pause, assess, then act. No rushed decisions. No fear-driven exits. Just a steady hand."

This gives clients a framework for managing future volatility — and positions you as the stabiliser, not the salesperson.

The real challenge with overreaction bias isn't stopping the emotion — it's making sure the emotion doesn't get to drive the strategy. When you offer perspective instead of panic, clients don't just stay invested — they stay empowered.

Herd Behaviour: The Gravitational Pull of Collective Action

A long queue forms outside a new restaurant in town. People walking by who had no intention of eating there start to wonder if they should join the queue too—after all, if that many people are waiting, it must be good.

Herd behaviour reveals a profound aspect of human psychology—our fundamental tendency to follow the crowd, even when individual logic might suggest otherwise. In financial markets, this bias manifests as a powerful collective movement that can drive entire investment trends, create market bubbles, and lead investors far from rational decision-making.

The evolutionary roots of herd behaviour are ancient. In prehistoric environments, following the group often meant survival. When faced with uncertainty, our brains are wired to seek safety in collective action. In modern financial markets, this instinct can transform from a survival mechanism to a significant cognitive trap.

From Concept to Conversation: Reframing the Crowd Mentality

Herd behaviour is rarely about the facts — it's about the *feeling of safety in numbers*. When clients see others moving en masse — whether into property, tech stocks, gold, or cash — the pull to follow can feel instinctive, even urgent.

Your job isn't to shame that instinct, but to reframe it. To help clients recognise the difference between shared wisdom and shared panic — and to anchor them back to their own plan.

Validate the pull of the crowd without endorsing it

"It's completely normal to wonder if others know something you don't. We're wired to trust group movement, especially in uncertain times."

Invite the client to zoom out

"Crowds can be right in the short term and very wrong in the long term. What matters is whether their direction matches your destination."

Reconnect to the personal plan

"Your financial plan wasn't built on what others are doing — it was built around what *you* value, what *you* want, and how much risk *you're* comfortable taking."

Use narrative to reverse the herd

"If we were sitting here in five years and the popular trade of today had completely unravelled, how would you feel if you'd jumped in just because everyone else was?"

Offer a mental benchmark

"When we notice a surge in investor enthusiasm or fear, that's often a sign to pause — not to pile in. The crowd might be running, but that doesn't mean they're running in the right direction."

As Warren Buffett famously put it:

"Be fearful when others are greedy, and greedy when others are fearful."

The crowd can be comforting — but that doesn't make it correct. Long-term investors aren't looking for company — they're looking for clarity. Your role is to help your client hold their ground when others lose theirs.

Mental Accounting: The Psychological Compartmentalisation of Money

Many people spend money differently when they are on holiday. Money set aside as "holiday cash" is spent much more freely than regular income, even though it all comes from the same bank account.

Mental accounting exposes a fascinating quirk of human psychology—our tendency to categorise money into different mental compartments, each with its own set of emotional rules. This bias leads people to treat money differently based on its perceived origin or intended purpose, often resulting in financially irrational decisions.

A powerful example of mental accounting in action is the way we respond to savings, depending on the size of the purchase. Let me share a story I often use with clients to bring this idea to life.

From Concept to Conversation: Naming the Hidden Rules

Mental accounting isn't just a financial quirk — it's a storytelling pattern clients don't realise they're following. They label pots of money with emotional meanings: "holiday cash," "bonus money," "untouchable savings." These labels feel real, but they aren't rational. And unless they're surfaced and gently questioned, they can shape client decisions in ways that quietly undermine their goals.

This is where story becomes your greatest tool.

Rather than telling a client they're thinking irrationally, show them how their own thinking works. Ask a question. Set a scene. Let them walk into the realisation — not because you told them, but because they recognised themselves in the story.

The next time a client shrugs off a small saving or labels a pot of money as "not worth worrying about," use a relatable scenario — like the value of saving £100 — to reveal the emotional logic behind the decision. Because once a client sees the pattern, they can begin to rewrite the rules.

The £100 Story: A Conversation About How Our Minds Trick Us

"It's only 0.75%, Mike," a client said to me once, smiling as he looked over the numbers I'd laid out on the table. "Hardly worth worrying about, is it?" I smiled back and said, "Can I tell you a quick story?"

He nodded.

"Picture yourself shopping for a new lamp for your living room," I said. "You find the perfect one — great size, right style — and it's £200. As you're queuing up to pay, you check your phone and spot the exact same lamp, just a few miles down the road, for £100. Half price."

"What would you do?" I asked him.

"I'd be off down the road in a flash!" he laughed.

"Of course you would. Most people would."

"Now imagine you're buying a new bathroom suite — a big-ticket item — £6,000. You find the perfect one, have a coffee to think about it, and while you're sitting there, you check your phone. Same suite, just a mile away, £5,900."

I paused. "Would you still drive across town to save £100?" He thought about it. "Honestly? Probably not."

"Same £100," I said. "Same few miles away. Same effort. But suddenly it feels smaller, right?"

He nodded slowly.

"That's how our minds play tricks on us," I said. "It's exactly why behavioural experts use the term 'mental accounting' — we label money differently depending on the situation, even though it's all the same."

"But money doesn't care what label we stick on it. It just grows — or it doesn't."

"Saving 0.75% on your investment costs every year might feel like nothing today. But over the years? It could mean tens of thousands — even hundreds of thousands — of pounds more in your pocket, instead of slowly leaking away."

"Wealth isn't built on one grand gesture. It's built on small, consistent, rational decisions. One £100 decision at a time." He smiled again – but this time, it was different. The penny had dropped.

Mental accounting is just one example of how our emotions quietly distort rational financial decisions. Another, equally powerful distortion happens when we start believing that past patterns somehow dictate future outcomes — a trap known as the Gambler's Fallacy.

Gambler's Fallacy: Misunderstanding Probability

A coin lands on heads five times in a row. The next time it is flipped, someone insists that it must land on tails because it is "due" for a change. But the reality is that each flip is independent—the odds are always 50/50.

The gambler's fallacy exposes a fundamental misunderstanding of probability that can devastate financial decision-making. Humans have an innate desire to find patterns, to believe that past events somehow influence future outcomes, even when mathematical probability proves otherwise.

From Concept to Conversation: Breaking the Illusion of Pattern

The gambler's fallacy appeals to something very human: the need for things to feel balanced. Clients might not talk in terms of "odds" or "randomness," but they often say things like:

"It's been going down for months — it's bound to bounce soon."
"This fund has had a great run — it's probably due for a correction."

They're trying to find fairness in what is often random — assigning cause-and-effect logic to events that are independent. Your job isn't to dismantle that instinct with cold logic, but to gently introduce clarity in the form of context.

Challenge the myth, not the person

"It's easy to feel like something's 'due' to happen — we're wired to see patterns. But the market doesn't work like a coin toss. It doesn't remember what happened last quarter, and it doesn't owe us a result."

Re-centre around process, not prediction

"The reason we follow a disciplined process is because markets are unpredictable. We don't need to guess what comes next — we just need to stick with a strategy that works over time."

Use relatable language

"If we saw a roulette wheel land on black five times in a row, it's tempting to bet on red — but the odds haven't changed. The wheel doesn't remember what came before. The odds reset to 37 to 1 on every spin. Investing has the same illusion. Just because something's been rising or falling doesn't mean it's due for a reversal."

Shift focus from timing to alignment

"Our goal isn't to call the next move. It's to make sure the decisions we're making today still align with where you're trying to go. That's how you win — not by guessing, but by staying aligned."

The gambler's fallacy tempts clients to see meaning in randomness. When you help them let go of the need for timing and focus instead on alignment, you don't just protect their portfolio — you protect their peace of mind.

Anchoring: The Tyranny of First Impressions

A shopper sees a jacket priced at £300. Later, they find another jacket for £150 and think, "What a bargain!" Even if the second jacket is still expensive, the mind has anchored to the first price, making the second one seem like a great deal.

Anchoring bias reveals how powerfully the first piece of information we receive can distort subsequent decision-making. In financial contexts, this might mean an investor fixates on the price they originally paid for a stock, refusing to sell it at a loss, even when objective analysis suggests it's no longer a sound investment.

From Concept to Conversation: Resetting the Reference Point

Anchoring bias happens fast and sticks deep. Whether it's the original share price, a market high, or what a friend paid for a similar investment, the first number a client encounters often becomes the mental benchmark — even if it's outdated or irrelevant.

Your job isn't to argue with the anchor — it's to gently help the client refocus on what actually matters.

Acknowledge how natural anchoring is

"It makes sense that the first price we see sticks with us — our brains are trying to find something to compare against. The challenge is that sometimes the first number we grab onto has nothing to do with what's actually right for us now."

Use narrative framing to flip perspective

When a client asks, *"Should I hold onto this investment?"*, and you sense they're anchored to the price they paid, you might say:

"Let me offer you a different way to think about this. Imagine someone walked in today and said, 'I'm thinking of adding this investment to my portfolio because it used to be worth more.' Would that feel like a strong reason to buy it?"

Pause — and let them reflect

You're not giving them a new answer. You're giving them a new lens. One that helps them see whether the original price is guiding their decision, rather than their goals.

Then say:

"We're not trying to guess what happens next — we're trying to make sure every decision still aligns with your plan. Anchoring to the price you paid can quietly get in the way of that."

Reframe anchors as history, not direction

"The price you paid gives us the starting point of the story — not the strategy. What matters now is where you want to go, and whether this investment still serves that journey."

Anchoring bias is sticky, but not permanent. When you help clients shift their reference point from the past to their future, you give them permission to let go of emotional baggage — and to make decisions rooted in purpose, not memory.

Overconfidence Bias: The Illusion of Superiority

A driver who has been on the road for years without an accident believes they are far superior behind the wheel compared to the average motorist. Because of this, they take unnecessary risks, assuming they are less likely to make mistakes.

Overconfidence bias is perhaps one of the most insidious psychological mechanisms in financial decision-making. Investors tend to overestimate their own abilities, knowledge, or control over outcomes. This can lead them to believe they can time the market perfectly or pick the best stocks — often resulting in excessive risks and frequent, costly trading.

This isn't unique to investing. In a well-known study, over 90% of drivers rated themselves as above-average behind the wheel — a statistical impossibility. It's a vivid reminder of how easily we fall into the trap of overestimating our own skill — especially in familiar or high-stakes environments.

These psychological biases are not flaws to be ashamed of, but natural human mechanisms to be understood and navigated. By recognising these patterns, investors can develop more thoughtful, measured approaches to financial decision-making.

The true art of financial advising lies not in eliminating these biases, but in helping clients understand and work with them — transforming potential psychological pitfalls into opportunities for more intentional financial choices.

From Concept to Conversation: Calming the Illusion of Control

Overconfidence doesn't always present as arrogance. More often, it sounds like conviction. Clients might say:

"I've got a good feel for the market."

"I've been watching things closely — I think it's time to move."

What they're expressing isn't foolishness. It's the deeply human need to feel in control — especially in uncertain times.

Affirm their engagement, but slow the leap

"I can see you've been paying close attention — that's great. The key is making sure our decisions stay grounded in your plan, not just what feels urgent right now." This acknowledges their thinking without reinforcing the urge to act.

Introduce the long-game lens

"One of the most consistent patterns I've seen is that the more frequently investors try to outguess the market, the more likely they are to underperform. It's not about whether we *can* act — it's about whether the action adds value over time."

This reframes confidence into discipline.

Invite them to step outside the emotion

"If someone close to you was considering making the same change you're thinking about — would you encourage them to do it?" This softens the emotional attachment and creates space for a more balanced response.

Reconnect with the plan

"Our job isn't to have perfect foresight — it's to keep making decisions that align with the outcomes you care most about. That's where real control lives."

Overconfidence isn't about ego — it's about how we cope with uncertainty. When you help clients slow down, reflect, and reconnect with their longer-term thinking, you turn overconfidence into composure — and create the space for smarter, steadier decisions.

Even with awareness of these biases, clients will still face moments of hesitation — emotional crossroads where logic and instinct pull in different directions. It's in these moments that the right story, question, or framing can make all the difference.

The Friend Mirror: A Tool for Crossroads Conversations

When clients are unsure — caught between instinct and reason, emotion, and action — there's one storytelling technique that consistently helps bring clarity. I call it *The Friend Mirror*.

It's simple, honest, and surprisingly powerful.

"Let's flip the situation for a moment. Knowing everything we know now, if our roles were reversed — and you were advising me, as a friend — what would you suggest I do?"

This isn't a manipulation. It's not a coaching trick. It's a behavioural reframing that gently invites the client to step outside their own emotional noise — and access a more grounded, value-led perspective.

Psychologists refer to this tendency as Solomon's Paradox — the observed phenomenon that people make wiser, less emotionally charged decisions when giving advice to others than when facing the same dilemma themselves. It's named after the biblical King Solomon, famous for dispensing wise counsel, but not always following it in his own life.

When clients are asked to imagine advising someone else — particularly someone they care about — they often pause. Their voice softens. Their response becomes more measured. In that moment, they hear their own wisdom — not from you, but from within themselves.

This isn't about cleverness — it's about integrity. The *Friend Mirror* reflects back who they want to be, not just how they feel in the moment.

And it works not just with one bias — but with *all* of them. Whether the client is gripped by loss aversion, overconfidence, herd behaviour, or anchoring, the Friend Mirror invites them to make the decision they would be proud of — not the one driven by impulse.

But biases don't exist in a vacuum. Every client arrives at your desk carrying not just their own internal psychology, but also the weight of their upbringing, culture, generational experience, and worldview. Their attitudes toward money, risk, and financial advice have been shaped over decades — often unconsciously — by the era they grew up in and the stories that defined it.

To truly connect with clients, you must understand more than their numbers and their goals. You must understand where they're coming from — historically, culturally, and emotionally.

Cultural and Generational Perspectives in Financial Storytelling

Financial narratives are never uniform. They are living, breathing ecosystems shaped by the intricate interplay of historical experiences, cultural conditioning, and individual perspectives. Each generation and cultural background brings a unique lens to understanding money, risk, and financial planning—a complex tapestry of inherited wisdom, collective memories, and personal aspirations.

The Generational Landscape of Financial Understanding

Different generations inhabit distinctly different financial universes. A client who grew up during an economic recession will approach financial planning with fundamentally different psychological mechanisms compared to someone who has only experienced periods of economic stability. These varied experiences create rich, nuanced narratives that demand careful, empathetic understanding.

Boomers: The Security Seekers

Baby Boomers, shaped by post-war economic optimism and subsequent periods of economic uncertainty, often prioritise financial stability above all else. Their financial stories are narratives of hard work, careful saving, and a deep-seated desire for economic security. They've witnessed significant economic transformations—from the prosperity of the 1950s to the economic challenges of subsequent decades—and their financial approach reflects these experiences.

For Boomers, financial advice is about preservation, protection, and creating a reliable safety net. They are more likely to value traditional investment approaches, long-term planning, and conservative strategies that minimise volatility and risk.

Generation X: The Pragmatic Navigators

Caught between the optimism of the Boomers and the digital fluency of Millennials, Generation X represents a bridge of financial adaptability. They have experienced significant economic shifts—witnessing the rise of personal computing, navigating multiple economic downturns, and developing a pragmatic approach to financial planning.

Their financial narratives are characterised by resilience, adaptability, and a more nuanced understanding of risk. Having seen both economic booms and significant market corrections, they approach financial planning with a balanced, somewhat cautious perspective.

Millennials: The Experiential Investors

Millennials bring an entirely different approach to financial decision-making. Shaped by economic uncertainty, student debt, and a digital-first worldview, they seek financial strategies that align with personal values, offer flexibility, and provide meaningful experiences.

Their financial storytelling is less about traditional wealth accumulation and more about creating a life of purpose. They are more likely to consider ethical investments, prioritise experiences over material possessions, and seek financial advice that speaks to their broader life goals.

Generation Z: The Digital Natives

For Generation Z, financial storytelling must be immediate, transparent, and aligned with technological innovation. They have grown up in a world of instant information, digital currencies, and rapidly changing economic landscapes. Their approach to money is fundamentally different—more fluid, more global, and more interconnected.

Cultural Dimensions of Financial Narratives

Beyond generational differences, cultural backgrounds profoundly shape financial understanding. Different cultures approach money, risk, and investment through unique philosophical and practical lenses:

- Asian cultures often prioritise family wealth and intergenerational planning
- Western cultures tend to emphasise individual financial independence
- Some cultures view debt as shameful, while others see it as a strategic tool
- Collective societies may approach financial decisions more communally, while individualistic cultures prioritise personal financial goals

Technological and Global Influences

In an increasingly interconnected world, financial contexts are becoming more global and technology driven. Emerging digital platforms, global investment opportunities, and instant access to information are reshaping how different generations and cultures understand and interact with financial concepts.

Crafting Adaptive Financial Narratives

The most effective financial advisers are those who can navigate these complex generational and cultural landscapes. They become linguistic translators, capable of crafting stories that resonate across different experiences and perspectives.

A single financial story might need multiple framings:

- For an older client, emphasise security and preservation
- For a younger investor, highlight growth and potential
- For a client from a collectivist culture, demonstrate how financial strategies support broader family goals

Conclusion: The Complexity of Financial Storytelling

Understanding these generational and cultural nuances transforms financial advising from a transactional interaction to a profound dialogue of human potential. It requires deep empathy, continuous learning, and a willingness to see beyond statistical models to the rich, complex human stories they represent.

Navigating Cognitive Dissonance in Financial Decision-Making

Financial beliefs are deeply personal narratives, intricate tapestries woven from threads of family experiences, cultural conditioning, and personal interactions with money. Cognitive dissonance emerges when new information challenges these long-held beliefs, creating a profound psychological tension that can paralyse financial decision-making.

The Anatomy of Financial Belief Systems

Every client arrives with a unique financial narrative, a complex ecosystem of inherited beliefs, emotional associations, and learned behaviours. These narratives are not simply rational constructs but living, breathing psychological landscapes that shape every financial choice.

The fundamental components of these financial belief systems include:

- Inherited beliefs passed down through family generations
- Cultural conditioning about wealth and risk
- Personal experiences of financial success or failure
- Deep-seated emotional associations with money
- Unconscious scripts that guide financial behaviours

These narratives operate beneath the surface of conscious awareness, creating invisible barriers that can prevent clients from making optimal financial decisions. They are the silent architects of financial choices, influencing everything from investment strategies to spending habits.

The Mirror Technique: A Gentle Approach to Narrative Transformation

Traditional approaches to challenging financial misconceptions often fail because they rely on confrontation and logical argument. The Mirror Technique offers a more nuanced pathway to helping clients recognise and overcome their ingrained financial beliefs.

Reflection Without Judgment

The core principle of the Mirror Technique is creating a safe, non-threatening space for self-exploration. This involves:

- Crafting stories that reflect the client's current financial behaviours
- Using neutral, observational language

- Illuminating potential consequences without direct criticism
- Allowing clients to see their financial patterns from a new perspective

Comparative Narrative Strategies

Effective narrative transformation requires a delicate balance of empathy and insight. By developing stories featuring characters who have successfully navigated similar financial misconceptions, advisers can create powerful opportunities for personal reflection.

A Practical Example: Rewriting Financial Narratives

Consider Maria's story—a narrative that illuminates the profound psychological journey of financial transformation:

"Maria believed saving was impossible with her current income. Years of family narratives about 'never having enough' had convinced her that financial security was for other people. Her internal dialogue was a constant refrain of limitation and scarcity.

The breakthrough came not through lectures or spreadsheets, but through a narrative that mirrored her own experiences while subtly expanding her perception of what was possible. By introducing her to a series of small, achievable saving strategies, we began to gently challenge her inherited belief system.

Small, consistent steps replaced the overwhelming narrative of scarcity with a new story of gradual financial empowerment. Each modest saving became an act of personal rebellion against the limiting beliefs she had internalised."

Strategies for Narrative Transformation

The most profound approach to overcoming cognitive dissonance requires:

- Creating emotional safety
- Introducing new perspectives gradually
- Practising empathetic listening
- Validating existing narratives
- Helping clients reframe their financial stories

The Psychology of Financial Belief Modification

Successful narrative intervention is an art form that demands:

- Deep empathy
- Extraordinary patience
- A non-confrontational approach
- Profound respect for the client's existing financial worldview

Cognitive Dissonance Resolution Checklist

Effective advisers constantly interrogate their approach:

- Have I truly validated the client's current financial narrative?
- Am I offering alternative perspectives without judgment?
- Does my story provide a bridge between existing beliefs and new possibilities?
- Have I created genuine emotional safety for exploring new financial concepts?

Conclusion: The Transformative Power of Narrative

By understanding and gently navigating cognitive dissonance, financial advisers become more than technical experts. They become trusted guides who help clients break free from limiting financial narratives, transforming deeply ingrained beliefs into opportunities for growth and financial empowerment.

The most powerful financial advice transcends numbers—it rewrites personal stories of possibility, helping clients see beyond their current limitations to the rich potential of their financial futures.

The Role of Timing and Relevance in Storytelling

In the delicate art of financial storytelling, timing is not just a consideration—it is the very heartbeat of effective communication. The right story, told at the wrong moment, can fall flat, while a seemingly simple narrative delivered at precisely the right instant can transform a client's entire financial perspective.

The Psychological Landscape of Narrative Timing

Timing in financial storytelling is a nuanced dance of emotional intelligence and strategic insight. It requires an almost intuitive understanding of a client's current life circumstances, emotional state, and receptiveness to new financial perspectives.

Every client interaction exists within a unique contextual moment—a confluence of personal experiences, current challenges, and future aspirations. The most impactful financial stories are those that speak directly to the client's immediate lived experience, creating an instant, visceral connection that transcends traditional advisory interactions.

Key Moments for Strategic Storytelling

Financial advisers must develop a keen sense of when stories can be most transformative:

Life Transitions: Windows of Receptivity

Major life events create natural openings for meaningful financial narratives. These are moments of heightened awareness and potential change:

- Marriage and partnership
- Buying a first home
- Preparing for or experiencing parenthood
- Approaching retirement
- Experiencing significant career shifts
- Losing a loved one

During these transitions, clients are naturally more open to new perspectives. A well-crafted story can help them navigate these complex emotional and financial landscapes, providing both practical guidance and emotional reassurance.

Market Volatility: Narrative as Emotional Anchor

Periods of economic uncertainty create unique storytelling opportunities. When markets fluctuate and anxiety runs high, clients seek more than just technical analysis. They need narratives that provide context, perspective, and emotional stability.

A story about previous market downturns and subsequent recoveries can transform panic into patience. By situating current challenges within a broader historical context, advisers can help clients maintain perspective and avoid reactive decision-making.

Financial Milestones: Celebrating and Projecting

Annual reviews and significant financial achievements create powerful moments for narrative reflection. These are opportunities to:

- Celebrate progress
- Contextualise past achievements
- Project future possibilities
- Reinforce the client's financial journey

The Anatomy of a Perfectly Timed Story

A strategically delivered financial narrative possesses several critical qualities:

- Immediate relevance to the client's current circumstances
- Emotional resonance that goes beyond mere numerical analysis
- A clear connection between past experiences and future possibilities
- Sufficient specificity to feel authentic
- Enough universality to be broadly relatable

Practical Example: Setting the Scene During Market Uncertainty

Consider a client, John, who is feeling nervous about a recent market downturn. The perfectly timed story might unfold like this:

"John, imagine it's 2008. The financial crisis is making headlines, and investors everywhere are feeling panicked. But those who stayed the course and didn't make knee-jerk reactions saw their portfolios recover and grow over the next decade. In fact, the market has historically rebounded from every downturn. Right now, it might feel uncertain, but by staying focused on the long-term plan we've created, you're positioning yourself to benefit when the market stabilises."

This narrative does more than provide information. It offers:

- Historical context
- Emotional reassurance
- A perspective that transcends immediate anxiety
- A sense of personal agency and control

The Subtle Art of Listening

Truly masterful timing requires deep listening. Before crafting a story, advisers must attune themselves to:

- The client's current emotional state
- Underlying concerns not explicitly stated
- Subtle cues that indicate readiness for new perspectives
- The broader life context surrounding financial decisions

Timing as a Strategic Instrument

Timing in financial storytelling is an art form that combines psychological insight, historical understanding, and a profound respect for individual human experience. It transforms financial advice from a transactional interaction to a meaningful dialogue about possibility, security, and personal potential.

The most effective financial advisers are those who understand that a story is not just about what is said, but when and how it is delivered. They become maestros of narrative timing, crafting stories that resonate at precisely the right moment, illuminating paths forward with wisdom, empathy, and strategic insight.

Balancing Facts with Fiction to Enhance Engagement

The art of financial storytelling resides in a delicate balance between empirical truth and narrative imagination. While facts provide the scaffolding of financial advice, fiction breathes life into these structures, transforming dry information into compelling human experiences that resonate deeply with clients.

The Power of Narrative Imagination

Financial concepts are inherently abstract. Numbers, market trends, and investment strategies exist in a realm of intellectual understanding that can feel distant and impersonal. Fiction serves as a bridge, translating these abstract ideas into tangible, relatable scenarios that clients can visualise and emotionally connect with.

Consider the difference between presenting a client with a spreadsheet of potential investment returns and sharing a story of a character who navigated similar financial challenges. The story invites the client into a lived experience, allowing them to mentally simulate the journey, understand the potential outcomes, and see themselves within the narrative.

Crafting Fictional Scenarios with Integrity

The key to effective narrative blending lies in maintaining absolute integrity. Fictional elements must be:

- Grounded in real-world possibilities
- Reflective of genuine financial principles
- Constructed to illuminate, not mislead
- Carefully balanced with factual underpinnings

A well-crafted fictional scenario is not an escape from reality, but a lens that brings financial complexity into sharper focus.

Practical Approaches to Narrative Blending Using Fiction to Simplify Complex Ideas

Imagine explaining diversification through a simple yet powerful metaphor. Instead of discussing asset allocation in technical terms, you might craft a story about a gardener who plants various crops to ensure a reliable harvest. Some plants might struggle in a given season, but the diversity ensures overall stability.

This approach transforms an abstract financial concept into a vivid, memorable experience. The client no longer hears a lecture about investment strategy but experiences a narrative that makes the principle intuitively understandable.

Real-World Inspiration: Fictional Interpretation

The most compelling financial stories often draw inspiration from actual client experiences while preserving individual privacy. By creating composite characters that blend multiple real-world scenarios, advisers can craft narratives that feel authentic and specific.

For instance, if you're explaining the risks of ignoring diversification, you might create a character like Jane. Her story might be a composite of several clients who faced similar challenges:

"Jane, a passionate tech professional, became enamoured with the booming technology sector. Inspired by stories of incredible startup successes, she invested almost all her savings in a single promising company. When that company experienced an unexpected downturn, Jane faced substantial losses that could have been mitigated through a more diversified approach."

Navigating Ethical Boundaries

While fiction can be a powerful storytelling tool, it comes with significant ethical responsibilities:

- Always clarify when a story is illustrative rather than literal
- Ensure fictional scenarios represent realistic possibilities
- Avoid creating unrealistic expectations
- Maintain transparency about the narrative's purpose

Balancing Techniques

1. **Start with Facts:** Ground your narrative in verifiable financial principles
2. **Introduce Narrative Elements:** Use fictional scenarios to illustrate these principles
3. **Return to Factual Context:** Provide clear, real-world implications

The Narrative Bridge

Balancing facts with fiction is an art form that transforms financial advice from a transactional interaction to a meaningful dialogue. It recognises that behind every financial decision are human hopes, fears, and aspirations.

The most effective financial advisers are storytellers who understand that numbers tell a story, but stories make numbers meaningful. They create narratives that don't just explain financial concepts but invite clients into a deeper understanding of their own financial potential.

The Swan Ice Sculpture: A Metaphor for the Impact of Inflation

The story of the swan ice sculpture is a powerful metaphor that captures the insidious nature of inflation—a silent force that gradually transforms and ultimately destroys financial potential.

Imagine a lavish wedding celebration. As you arrive, impeccably dressed, you're greeted by a breathtaking centrepiece—a magnificent swan ice sculpture. At first glance, it is a work of art, pristine and perfect. The intricate details are stunning: every feather carefully carved, the beak precisely defined. It stands as a symbol of beauty, elegance, and momentary perfection.

When you first arrive, the sculpture is an absolute marvel. The definition is exquisite—you can see every delicate line, every nuanced curve. The accompanying drip tray beneath it is completely empty, suggesting absolute perfection and control.

As the wedding celebration progresses, something subtle yet profound begins to happen. Return to the sculpture an hour later, and you'll notice the first signs of transformation. The drip tray now contains a small amount of water. The sculpture's edges have softened almost imperceptibly. The once-crisp details are beginning to blur.

By the time the evening reaches its later stages, the transformation is dramatic. What was once a stunning, precise work of art has become barely recognisable. The swan has melted into an undefined block of ice, and the drip tray is now completely full of water. The magnificent creation has been reduced to a mere puddle, its former glory completely eroded.

The Deeper Metaphorical Landscape

This ice sculpture serves as a profound metaphor for inflation's quiet destruction of financial value. Just as the sculpture melts away, seemingly without dramatic intervention, inflation slowly but relentlessly erodes purchasing power. The process is so gradual that it often goes unnoticed until significant damage has occurred.

Most individuals fail to perceive inflation's impact because its destruction happens incrementally. Each moment seems insignificant—a slight softening here, a barely perceptible change there. But over time, these small changes accumulate into massive transformations.

The Psychological Dimensions of Financial Erosion

The swan ice sculpture analogy speaks to something deeper than mere financial mathematics. It reveals the psychological experience of financial value erosion. Just as wedding guests might be momentarily distracted, failing to notice the sculpture's gradual destruction, investors often remain unaware of inflation's persistent impact.

This metaphor invites a profound reflection on the nature of value. What appears solid and unchanging is, in reality, constantly transforming. The swan represents our financial aspirations—carefully crafted, seemingly permanent—while the melting process symbolises the relentless economic forces that challenge those aspirations.

Practical Implications

The lesson is clear: financial strategies must account for this gradual erosion. Merely preserving money is not enough. Investments must not only maintain value but outpace inflation's destructive potential.

Just as a skilled event planner might place the ice sculpture in a controlled environment or replace it periodically, investors must continually manage their financial plans. This means:

- Seeking investments that provide returns that at least keep pace with inflation
- Regularly reviewing and adjusting financial strategies
- Understanding that preservation requires active, thoughtful management

Embracing Financial Resilience

The swan ice sculpture is more than a metaphor—it is an invitation to financial mindfulness. It challenges investors to look beyond momentary appearances, to understand the subtle yet powerful forces that shape financial realities.

By recognising inflation's gradual erosion, investors can transform from passive observers to active architects of their financial futures. The most successful financial journeys are those that anticipate and adapt to these quiet, persistent changes.

Just as the wedding guests might pause to truly observe the sculpture's transformation, investors must cultivate a similar awareness—watching, understanding, and strategically responding to the economic forces that shape their financial landscape.

Making Context the Cornerstone of Effective Financial Storytelling

Context is the lifeblood of meaningful financial communication. It transforms abstract numerical concepts into living, breathing narratives that resonate deeply with human experience. By grounding advice in real-world events, blending facts with fiction, and timing stories to align with clients' circumstances, financial advisers create narratives that clients can see themselves within and feel inspired by.

The Transformative Power of Contextual Storytelling

The most profound financial advice transcends mere numbers. It becomes a bridge between technical knowledge and human aspiration, connecting cold calculations to deeply personal hopes and fears. Context not only strengthens your story but also strengthens the trust and connection between you and your clients.

Financial narratives are never static documents to be filed away. They are dynamic conversations between possibility and preparedness. Each client brings a unique constellation of experiences—generational patterns, cultural influences, personal traumas, and unexpected moments of inspiration—that shape their financial worldview.

Navigating the Complexity of Financial Narratives

The art of financial storytelling demands a radical reimagining of how we communicate financial concepts. It requires moving beyond linear thinking, embracing uncertainty as a fundamental aspect of financial planning. The most effective financial advisers are those who can navigate this complexity with empathy, insight, and a profound respect for the individual's unique journey.

Imagine financial storytelling as a form of cartography. You are not drawing fixed maps but creating adaptable navigational tools. You are not predicting the future but preparing for its inherent uncertainty. Through your stories, you help clients develop a kind of financial resilience that goes beyond mere numbers—a resilience rooted in self-understanding, emotional intelligence, and the capacity to adapt.

The Delicate Balance of Narrative Creation

The true art of financial storytelling lies in a delicate balance: providing structure and guidance while simultaneously honouring the unpredictable, deeply personal nature of each individual's financial journey. It is about creating narratives that are at once grounded and expansive, practical, and inspirational.

As financial advisers, your role is not to simplify or reduce these complex stories, but to illuminate their nuanced beauty. You are translators, helping clients understand the rich, multifaceted language of their own financial potential.

Preparing for the Next Chapter of Financial Understanding

Context is more than a storytelling technique—it is a fundamental approach to understanding financial decisions. By mastering contextual storytelling, you transform financial advice from a transactional interaction to a meaningful dialogue about possibility, security, and personal potential.

In the next chapter, we will explore how to use storytelling to simplify complex financial concepts, helping clients feel empowered to make informed decisions without feeling overwhelmed. This step is crucial in ensuring that your clients not only understand but truly embrace the financial strategies that will support their goals.

A Final Reflection

Every financial story is a journey of human potential. It is about more than money—it is about dreams, security, legacy, and the profound human capacity to imagine and create a better future. As you continue to develop your skills in contextual storytelling, remember that your most powerful tool is not your technical expertise, but your ability to listen, understand, and translate complex financial realities into meaningful personal narratives.

Context is king, but empathy is the true power behind the throne.

FIVE KEY TAKEAWAYS

1. Context is essential in financial storytelling as it transforms abstract numerical concepts into relatable narratives that help clients understand the relevance of financial advice to their personal situations.

2. Different generations (Boomers, Gen X, Millennials, Gen Z) approach financial planning with unique perspectives based on their lived experiences, requiring advisers to adapt their storytelling to resonate with each group's specific worldview.

3. Psychological biases like recency bias, prospect theory, and herd behaviour significantly influence financial decision-making, and understanding these biases helps advisers guide clients toward more rational choices.

4. Effective financial communication requires balancing factual information with narrative elements that make complex concepts accessible, memorable, and emotionally engaging for clients.

5. Timing is critical when delivering financial stories—certain moments such as life transitions, market volatility, or financial milestones create natural openings when clients are more receptive to new financial perspectives.

CHAPTER 6

Simplifying Complex Concepts with Stories

―――――◇―――――

"Simplicity is the ultimate sophistication"
—*Leonardo da Vinci*

Let me share a secret about financial communication that took me years to learn. It's not about impressing clients with complicated jargon or overwhelming them with technical details. It's about speaking a language they understand - the language of stories. It's not about being the smartest person in the room, because if you think you are, you are probably in the wrong room.

Your job is to simplify, simplify, simplify. Financial jargon can be overwhelming for clients, and complex terms often stand in the way of clear understanding. By using analogies and relatable examples, you can transform intimidating concepts into familiar ideas that clients grasp easily. Simplifying doesn't mean dumbing down; it means distilling ideas, so clients feel informed and empowered.

Think of financial advising as translating a foreign language. A well-crafted analogy is like a bridge that connects your knowledge with your client's understanding. Imagine explaining pensions as wells: if you keep drawing water without allowing the well to refill, it will eventually run dry. This illustrates why pacing pension withdrawals is essential, making a potentially complex concept straightforward.

Have you ever watched someone's eyes glaze over when you start talking about financial concepts? "Asset allocation," "liquidity," "pensions," "diversification" - these words might as well be a foreign language. They create an instant barrier, pushing clients away instead of drawing them closer.

I have spoken with thousands of clients over the years, and I have never met a single person who was remotely interested in a pension; however, they were all very interested in future spending money. Clients don't dream about pensions, they dream about the experiences, adventures, and choices those pensions will enable.

How did you learn your most important life lessons? Probably not from dry textbooks or complicated charts, right? We humans are visual creatures. We understand the world through stories, through images that help complex ideas make sense.

Financial advisers often forget this. We get caught up in numbers, percentages, and complicated graphs. But what if I told you that a simple sketch could explain more than pages of technical analysis? Most people learn visually—yet financial advisers often rely only on words. Simple sketches and diagrams can dramatically improve comprehension.

The Power of a Simple Picture

Imagine a timeline for retirement planning. It's not just a line with some points. It's a personal journey of financial potential. Each point tells a chapter of your clients' life story. The early years? That's about planting seeds of investment. Mid-career becomes a time of careful cultivation. As retirement approaches, they're harvesting the fruits of their patient planning.

A bar chart showing compound interest isn't just a bunch of rectangles. It's a visual story of financial transformation. Watch those bars start small, almost imperceptibly. Then, something magical happens. They begin to grow, building momentum, eventually showing a growth that seems almost miraculous.

Breaking Down Financial Jargon: Turning Complexity into Conversation

Financial language can feel like a maze of confusing terms. But every complicated concept has a simple story waiting to be told. Let me share a secret about explaining complex financial concepts: the most powerful tool isn't a complicated chart or a technical term. It's a simple story or analogy that helps people see something unfamiliar through the lens of something they can easily relate to.

The Snowball Effect in Numbers

Remember our snowball rolling down the mountain analogy from Chapter 2? Now let's see this powerful metaphor in action with real figures.

Earlier, we discussed how compound interest behaves just like that snowball—starting small but growing exponentially as it gathers momentum. What makes this concept so remarkable isn't just the imagery, but the mathematical reality behind it.

Let me introduce you to Emma and James to demonstrate the snowball effect with actual numbers:

- Emma starts investing £200 monthly at age 25
- James begins at age 35, investing £300 monthly

Despite James investing 50% more each month, the snowball principle reveals something astonishing. Assuming a 7% annual return over 40 years:

- Emma's total investment: £96,000
- James's total investment: £108,000
- Emma's final balance: Approximately £465,000
- James's final balance: Approximately £340,000

This is our snowball in action. Emma's ten-year head start results in £125,000 more wealth, despite investing £12,000 less. Just as we saw with our snowball metaphor, the early accumulation that seemed so modest initially created massive momentum over time.

The numbers powerfully illustrate what our snowball analogy teaches us about:

1. Starting early
2. The cost of delay
3. Compound interest
4. Time in the market

The Power of Compounding: The Incredible Growth of a Folded A4 Sheet of Paper

Because compounding is a concept that many people struggle to grasp, one of the most powerful ways to illustrate its exponential impact is by considering what happens if you could physically fold a piece of paper in half repeatedly.

Imagine taking a standard A4 sheet of paper, approximately 0.1mm thick, and folding it in half. If you could continue folding it 50 times, how tall do you think the final stack would be? Most people vastly underestimate the result.

Each time you fold the paper, its thickness doubles:

- 1st fold → 0.2mm
- 2nd fold → 0.4mm
- 3rd fold → 0.8mm
- 4th fold → 1.6mm (already thicker than a coin)

- 10th fold → 10.24cm (about the height of a coffee mug)
- 20th fold → 104m (higher than Big Ben)
- 30th fold → 107km (well into space!)
- 40th fold → 109,951km (a quarter of the way to the Moon)
- 50th fold → 112,589,991km (three-quarters the distance to the Sun!)

Yes, you read that correctly. If it were physically possible to fold a piece of paper 50 times, its height would reach over 112 million kilometres, taking it nearly to the Sun! To get your head around this—just one more fold, and it would reach the sun and back.

This mind-blowing example perfectly illustrates the power of exponential growth—the same principle that drives long-term investing. When money is left to grow with compound interest or investment returns, the gains themselves start generating further gains, much like each fold doubling the thickness of the paper.

The next time someone underestimates the power of compounding, ask them how far they think a folded piece of A4 paper would reach after 50 folds. I guarantee their answer will be miles off—literally! It's always a fun question to ask friends, as most people have no idea just how mind-blowing the result is.

Navigating Financial Oceans

For clients nervous about market changes, I love comparing an investment portfolio to a ship navigating the ocean. Some days will be calm, other days rough. But a well-constructed ship is designed to withstand these variations and reach its destination. Lifeboats are the strategies that help us navigate stormy seas.

Think about a skilled captain and the crew. They don't panic at the first sign of waves. They understand the journey involves ups and downs. They've prepared, they're flexible, and they keep their ultimate destination in mind.

Asset Allocation: Cooking Up a Financial Strategy

Imagine you're preparing the perfect meal. A great chef doesn't just throw random ingredients together. They carefully select a balance of proteins, vegetables, grains - each bringing something unique to the table. Financial planning works exactly the same way.

Your investment portfolio is like a nutritious dinner plate. Stocks might be your protein - high-energy and growth-oriented. Bonds are your vegetables - steady and reliable. Cash is your grains - providing flexibility and foundational support. The magic isn't in any single ingredient, but in how they work together to create something nourishing.

Liquidity: Understanding Financial Accessibility

Think about money like different types of containers. Your wallet is an open container - cash you can grab instantly. A savings account is like a container with a quick-release lid. A fixed-term deposit? That's more of a locked box. Each container has its own rules about how quickly you can access what's inside.

The Emotional Landscape of Investing

Investing isn't just about numbers. It's a deeply personal journey that touches on our most fundamental hopes, fears, and dreams.

Consider Margaret, a client who grew up in a family that always spoke about money in hushed, anxious tones. For years, this shaped her approach to investing. She was terrified of making a wrong move, of losing what little she had. Our work together wasn't just about investment strategies. It was about helping her rewrite her financial narrative.

Our relationships with money often run deeper than we realise. They're inherited stories passed down through generations. Some families see money as a source of security, others as a means of opportunity. Some view wealth with suspicion, others with excitement.

Here's a truth many people don't understand: investing is an emotional journey. Market changes can trigger some of our deepest fears and most irrational impulses.

Picture this. You're watching your investments, and suddenly the numbers start to drop. Panic sets in. Your brain starts screaming, "Do something! Anything!" It's like being on a ship in a storm, and all you want to do is abandon ship. But here's the thing - that's exactly when most investors make their biggest mistakes. I tell my clients that my job isn't to talk them down from the ledge—it's to ensure they're informed enough never to feel the urge to climb up there in the first place.

The Dangerous Urge to Constantly Check

Modern technology has made financial anxiety even more challenging. Smartphone apps, real-time market updates - they're like a siren call, tempting you to constantly peek at your investments. It's like having a garden and digging up the seeds every single day to see if they're growing.

Imagine planting a delicate seedling. Every time you dig it up to check its roots, you're causing more damage than good. Investments are remarkably similar. They need consistent care, yes, but also the time to develop naturally.

Snakes and Ladders: The Stock Market Edition

The timeless game of Snakes and Ladders provides an apt analogy for the intricacies of stock market investing for clients. Just as in the game, investors aim to climb the ladder, steadily building their wealth through informed choices, diversification, and adherence to long-term strategies. The well-constructed ladders in our investing game represent stable, high-performing assets, like global equities. These ladders are the instruments of steady, sustainable growth.

However, just as we find in the game, there are snakes lurking. These pitfalls are not always obvious, and they can derail even the most experienced investors. They embody the perils of media noise, a tumultuous whirlwind of opinions, speculations, and sometimes baseless predictions that can lead an investor astray. Investing based on emotions, or the latest media buzz is akin to landing on the snake's head, with a rapid slide down, away from one's financial goals.

Another snake is our very own behavioural biases. These intrinsic patterns of decision-making can push us to act on impulse, favouring short-term gains over long-term stability, or making decisions based on past experiences rather than current data. Such biases can be a silent saboteur, waiting to send an investor tumbling back down.

It's worth noting that while the stock market isn't a game, understanding its Snakes and Ladders nature can equip investors with a perspective that emphasises patience, resilience, and continuous learning.

And just like the game, with the right strategy and a bit of luck, the ultimate prize—a robust financial future—is within reach. But always remember, a wise player knows when to sidestep the snakes and when to take the next step up a ladder.

The Rollercoaster of Market Volatility

Let me paint you a vivid picture. Imagine lining up for a rollercoaster ride. There's anticipation, a hint of anxiety. As you climb higher, your heart races. The descent is breathtaking - full of loops and turns that make you want to scream, "I need to get off!"

But here's the crucial lesson: any attempt to exit during the ride would lead to catastrophic outcomes. You stay put, weathering the ups and downs, knowing the ride will eventually end.

This is exactly how market volatility works. Understanding and sticking to your investment strategy during these market loops is crucial. Exiting during downturns means missing potential recoveries - like getting off the rollercoaster at its lowest point.

The legendary investor Howard Marks said something profound: "Volatility can be seen as a mere indicator of risk presence, but it does not constitute risk in its entirety." Think of it like a rollercoaster journey - the twists and turns aren't the whole story.

In a nutshell, most investors confuse volatility with permanent loss and this is extremely dangerous. You don't try to get out of a roller coaster when you are upside down mid loop the loop. The ups and downs represent volatility but getting out of your seat whilst upside results in permanent loss.

The Only Store Where People Run Away From Sales: The Psychology of Market Discounts

Financial adviser Rachel noticed a pattern with her prospective clients. When markets were rising steadily, her phone rang constantly with people eager to invest. But whenever markets dropped significantly, those same prospects would suddenly go quiet or postpone meetings.

During one particularly volatile week when markets had fallen nearly 15%, Rachel met with David, a surgeon who had been considering investing a significant sum from his practice's profits. She could see the hesitation in his eyes as they reviewed the latest market news.

"I'm thinking maybe we should wait until things settle down," David said, fidgeting with his pen. "It just doesn't feel like the right time with everything falling. What if it falls even further?"

Rachel nodded thoughtfully. "David, may I share an observation I've made over the years?"

He nodded, relief evident in his expression at the potential delay.

"The stock market is the only store I know where customers run away when everything goes on sale," Rachel said with a gentle smile. "Think about it for a moment. When your favourite clothing store has a 15% off sale, what do you do?"

"I suppose I'm more likely to shop there," David admitted.

"Exactly. And if they had a 30% off sale?"

"I'd probably buy even more."

Rachel leaned forward. "Yet when the market offers the exact same discounts on ownership of great businesses, most people have the opposite reaction—they run away in fear. Instead of seeing lower prices as an opportunity, they see them as a threat."

David looked thoughtful. "I never considered it that way before. But what if prices fall further after I invest? Wouldn't I be better off waiting for the bottom?"

"That's a common concern," Rachel acknowledged. "Think of it this way: If your favourite store offered 30% off today, would you refuse to buy because next week it might be 40% off? You might miss the sale entirely if prices return to normal. The Covid market decline in 2020 is a perfect example—the 'sale' only lasted about five months before markets not only recovered but reached new highs."

"The truth is nobody—not even the most successful investors—can consistently identify the absolute bottom of the market. What we do know is that quality investments purchased at a significant discount tend to reward patient investors over time."

David seemed to be considering this perspective. "That makes sense, but I'm still nervous."

Rachel nodded, sensing that while the idea had landed intellectually, David's emotions still weren't fully on board. That wasn't unusual. Fear rarely gives up after one conversation. She knew that when logic only half-convinces, it's often a shift in perspective — something visual, something relatable — that helps it take root. So, she offered a few more everyday analogies to bring the concept closer to home.

The Shopping Trolley Perspective

"Let me share another way to think about this," Rachel continued. "Imagine you're at your favourite department store, and you see that all your preferred brands are suddenly marked down 30%. Your favourite items that normally sell out quickly are available at prices you've never seen before."

"Would you fill your shopping trolley, or would you walk out empty-handed, thinking 'I'll wait until everything returns to full price'?"

David laughed. "Well, when you put it that way, I'd certainly fill my trolley."

"Exactly! Yet that's precisely what most investors do during market downturns. They avoid buying when quality investments are on sale, preferring instead to wait until prices have recovered—essentially choosing to pay full price rather than get a discount."

"But I've also considered just moving to cash until things settle down," David mentioned. "Just to protect what I have until the storm passes."

"That's another common reaction," Rachel said. "But let me share an analogy that might help you see the potential problem with that approach."

The House Sale Mistake

"Imagine you own a house that was valued at £500,000 last year. Suddenly, property prices in your area start falling dramatically. You watch anxiously as your home's value drops to £400,000—a 20% decline. Unable to stand the stress any longer, you decide to sell the house at £400,000, put the money in the bank, and wait for the market to stabilise before buying again."

"So, you sell for £400,000 and have that amount sitting in your bank account. You tell yourself, 'At least I've stopped the bleeding. I'll wait until things feel safer, then get back in.'"

"But then, as typically happens, the property market recovers over the following months. Your former home is now worth £525,000—even higher than when you originally owned it. Now you want to buy back in, but there's an obvious problem—you only have £400,000 in the bank. You can't afford to buy back the same house you previously owned."

David nodded slowly. "I'd be £125,000 short..."

"Exactly. By selling after the decline, you locked in a permanent loss and then completely missed the recovery. Had you simply stayed put through the downturn, you would still own a house now worth £525,000."

Rachel paused, letting the example sink in. "This is precisely what happens when investors move to cash during market downturns. They sell after experiencing the pain of the decline, make that temporary loss permanent, and then find themselves unable to fully participate in the recovery."

"When clients tell me they want to move to cash during market declines, I ask them three simple questions: Has your time horizon changed? Has your investment strategy changed? Have your long-term plans changed?"

David thought for a moment. "In my case, no to all three."

"Exactly. If the answers are no, then making a dramatic change based solely on recent market movements is classic recency bias in action—giving too much weight to what's happening right now and not enough to long-term fundamentals. It's making a permanent decision based on temporary circumstances."

The Car Showroom Conundrum

"Here's one final way to think about it," Rachel added, seeing that David was becoming more receptive. "Imagine you've been to a car showroom and test driven a car three times. The salesman knows you're very interested but can't quite commit."

"Then one day, you get a call telling you that due to new stock coming in, they're prepared to sell you the car at a 20% discount. Would you say, 'No thanks, I'll wait until it goes back to full price before I buy it'?"

David shook his head, smiling. "Of course not. That would be absurd."

Rachel smiled warmly. "It's funny how obvious it sounds when we talk about discounts in shops or car showrooms. But when it comes to investments, our emotions cloud everything."

"Let me share a quick real-world example. It's something I often tell clients who are nervous about investing during downturns."

"Imagine you own a beautiful watch. Not just any watch — a genuine luxury piece, worth £5,000. You've worn it, admired it, trusted it to hold its value over time."

"But then you hear rumours: 'The luxury watch market is cooling.' Prices are dipping. You check online — and sure enough, similar watches are being listed for £4,500."

"Panic creeps in. You worry: 'What if it drops even more? What if no one wants it soon?' So, you rush to a dealer and say, 'Take it off my hands. I'll accept £4,000.' The dealer — who knows full well that quality watches usually recover — smiles and shakes your hand."

"A few weeks later, the market stabilises. Your old watch is now selling for £5,500."

Rachel paused. "Who came out better?"

David chuckled ruefully. "Not the seller."

"Exactly. You didn't lose because the watch was worthless. You lost because you panicked. Meanwhile, the dealer — calm and patient — picked up a valuable asset at a huge discount. He's rubbing his hands together while you're nursing a loss."

"And that's exactly what happens in investing. When you sell a good investment cheaply out of fear, there's always someone else ready to scoop it up — and they're smiling all the way to the bank."

Rachel leaned back. "The moral is simple: just because something temporarily falls in value doesn't mean it's no longer worth owning. Often, it's quite the opposite."

David studied the chart again, seeing how the major market declines were followed by substantial recoveries. "So, you're suggesting this market drop is actually... a good thing for someone in my position?"

"Precisely," Rachel nodded. "Human psychology makes us fear loss about twice as much as we value equivalent gains. This 'loss aversion' leads to poor investment timing. We feel comfortable buying when markets are up because it seems safer, but that's actually when we're paying premium prices. The discomfort you're feeling right now? That's exactly the emotion that creates opportunity for disciplined investors."

Rachel then shared a real example from her practice. "During the 2008 financial crisis, I had a client who, against the prevailing fear, invested a substantial inheritance when markets were down about 40%. While everyone else was panicking, he understood he was buying ownership in great businesses at fire-sale prices. Within five years, that investment had nearly doubled. The short-term pain created a remarkable long-term opportunity."

David sat back, perspective visibly shifting. "I've been looking at this completely backwards, haven't I?"

"Most people do," Rachel assured him. "Our natural instincts around financial decisions often lead us astray. That's why having a thoughtful strategy—and sticking to it especially when it feels difficult—is so important."

Two days later, David called Rachel to proceed with his investment plan, with one adjustment—he wanted to invest a bit more than originally planned.

"After all," he said, "who doesn't like a good sale?"

Adviser Reflection

The "market sale" analogy resonates deeply because it highlights a fundamental disconnect in investor behaviour. By reframing market downturns as discount opportunities rather than reasons for fear, we help clients make decisions that align with their long-term interests rather than their short-term emotions.

This perspective shift doesn't eliminate the discomfort of volatile markets, but it gives clients a productive way to think about and respond to them. The shopping trolley, house sale and car dealership examples are particularly powerful because they make the illogical nature of waiting for higher prices immediately obvious, even to someone in the grip of loss aversion.

Of course, not every client reaction is about logic. Sometimes, what we're dealing with isn't a pricing misunderstanding — it's panic. Deep, visceral, fight-or-flight panic. And when fear takes over, analogies about sales and discounts often aren't enough. In those moments, clients don't need numbers — they need perspective. And perhaps nothing illustrates the danger of reacting to fear better than what I call *the burning theatre.*

The Burning Theatre: A Story About Panic and Patience

Imagine you're sitting in a grand old theatre. The show is midway through. You've paid good money, your seat is comfortable, and the performance—though intense—is unfolding just as the director intended.

Then, someone in the back row jumps up. *"Smoke!"* they shout.

A ripple of panic surges through the audience. A few people stand. Some glance nervously at the exits. You look around. There's no fire. No alarm. But the mood has changed.

More people begin to move. The exits clog. Elbows fly. You feel the anxiety rising in your chest. The person beside you grabs their coat. And now the show—the reason you're here—is completely drowned out by the fear of what might happen.

This is the market in a crisis. Howard Marks once said that *"panicking out of the market and going into cash is the cardinal sin of investing."* Why? Because like bolting from a theatre at the first shout of smoke, it feels rational in the moment—but it's driven by fear, not facts.

And here's the moment of truth for every adviser. This is when the client turns to you—not for charts, not for 100-year return graphs—but for something far more human. Reassurance. Meaning. A story that steadies the heart.

Yet what do most advisers do? They pull out performance data. They start talking about averages and compound returns. But here's the problem: your client isn't sitting in a lecture hall. They're sitting in that theatre, and the smoke feels real.

And this is where storytelling becomes your greatest asset. Because in that moment, your client is likely saying:

"I know markets recover. But this time feels different." And they're right—*every crisis feels different*. That's what makes it a crisis.

So, what do you do? You meet emotion with story.

You might say:

"I once worked with a couple in 2008 who felt just like this. They were two weeks from selling everything and going to cash. We had a conversation, not about returns, but about why they invested in the first place. We reconnected with their goals, not the headlines. And they stayed in. A decade later, their portfolio had more than doubled—but more importantly, they never forgot what it meant to hold their nerve when it counted." That story doesn't just inform—it transforms. Because when panic strikes, data doesn't calm people. Stories do.

And in that burning theatre of fear, you don't win trust by shouting back facts. You win it by being the calm voice that says, *"Stay seated. The show isn't over. And this isn't the first time someone shouted fire when there wasn't one."*

Most importantly, this framing helps clients understand that temporary discomfort can create lasting opportunity—a lesson that separates successful long-term investors from those who consistently buy high and sell low, often as a result of misplaced panic.

Our clients don't need complex technical explanations about market cycles and valuation metrics. They need relatable analogies that transform their perception of market declines from threats to opportunities. When we succeed in shifting this perspective, we don't just help them make better investment decisions—we fundamentally change their relationship with market volatility, potentially improving their investment outcomes for decades to come.

Once a client's fear begins to soften, and they stop seeing every drop in the market as a personal threat, you can begin to introduce deeper distinctions—like the difference between risk and volatility. Because often, what they fear isn't true risk at all. It's just short-term movement wearing the mask of danger.

Risk vs Volatility is Like Weather vs Climate

Risk and volatility in investing are like the difference between weather and climate. Volatility is like the weather—it changes daily, and it can be unpredictable, with sunny days followed by storms. But risk is more like the climate—it's about the broader, long-term trends. Volatility might make the journey feel bumpy, but risk determines whether you reach your destination safely. Just as focusing too much on daily weather changes can distract from the overall climate pattern, reacting emotionally to short-term market movements can derail a long-term investment strategy.

During market downturns, fear often takes over, causing investors to make rash decisions. However, reacting emotionally to short-term market movements is usually a mistake. Understanding that volatility is a normal part of investing can help investors remain calm and stay the course. Clients should focus on the climate, not a rainy day.

Not Panicking When Tough Times Come is Like Turbulence on a Flight

Imagine you're on a turbulent flight. Some passengers panic at the first sign of turbulence, gripping their seats and fearing the worst. But experienced travellers know that turbulence is just part of flying—it's uncomfortable but rarely dangerous. In investing, the markets will inevitably experience ups and downs, but panicking during those tough times can lead to poor decisions, like selling at the worst possible moment. Staying calm and riding out the storm leads to smoother landings in the long run.

Navigating Life's Financial Uncertainties

Investing isn't a straight path to the top. It's more like a winding road with unexpected turns, occasional roadblocks, and some breathtaking views. Some years, clients will feel like they're cruising down a smooth highway. Other years, they'll be navigating through challenging terrain.

The investors who succeed aren't those who never face challenges. They're the ones who understand that setbacks are part of the journey. Just like life itself, investing presents both opportunities to move forward and moments that might push you backward. Success depends on how we navigate these moments.

The Tools of Financial Navigation

Think of yourself as a financial explorer. You're not just managing money - you're charting a course through complex economic landscapes. Your most powerful tools aren't complicated spreadsheets or high-tech algorithms. They're patience, understanding, temperament, and the ability to see the bigger picture.

A simple whiteboard can become a canvas for financial storytelling. A tablet drawing app can transform complex ideas into visual journeys. But the most important tool? Your ability to help clients see beyond the immediate moment and understand their true financial potential.

Technology: A Supportive Companion, Not a Master

Financial technology has given us remarkable tools - apps that track market movements, algorithms predicting potential investments, real-time data at our fingertips. But here's the crucial insight: these are tools that enhance, not replace, human understanding.

A computer cannot grasp the emotional nuances behind financial decisions. It cannot recognise the personal stories that shape investment choices. This is where human insight becomes invaluable.

Imagine technology as a powerful pair of binoculars. They help you see further, understand more clearly, but they don't replace the wisdom of the explorer using them. Interactive platforms, augmented reality simulations - these are amplifiers of human connection, making complex financial concepts more tangible and engaging.

The Art of Perspective

Successful investing isn't about being perfect. It's about being thoughtful. It's about creating a strategy that can adapt, grow, and weather various financial conditions. Every setback is a learning opportunity. Every challenge is a chance to understand yourself and your financial journey better.

Remember the words of the legendary investor Warren Buffett: "Someone's sitting in the shade today because someone planted a tree a long time ago." Your financial decisions today are the trees you're planting for your future self.

The Dance of Risk and Opportunity

Get clients to imagine investing as a complex dance. Sometimes they're leading, sometimes they're following. Sometimes the music is smooth and predictable, other times it's all wild and unpredictable. But the key is to keep moving, to stay balanced, and to enjoy the rhythm.

Risk isn't something to be feared. It's something to be understood, respected, and carefully navigated. Think of it like crossing a beautiful but challenging mountain path. You wouldn't charge blindly ahead, but you also wouldn't let fear keep you from the incredible view.

Beyond the Numbers

Here's a profound truth: financial planning is about far more than money. It's about dreams. It's about creating possibilities. It's about giving clients and their loved ones the freedom to live the life they truly want.

An investment isn't just a number on a spreadsheet. It's a seed of potential. It's a promise to your future self. It's a way of saying, "I believe in what's possible."

A Conversation, Not a Lecture

The best financial advice doesn't come from a place of superiority. It comes from a place of partnership. Of understanding. Of recognising that every person's financial journey is unique and deeply personal.

An adviser should be more like a trusted friend than a distant expert. Someone who listens. Who asks questions. Who helps you see possibilities you might have missed. Great financial advice is storytelling. It's about helping clients see their financial journey as a narrative of possibility, not a series of cold calculations. When you turn complex ideas into stories that feel personal and meaningful, that's when real understanding happens—and trust is built.

Crafting Your Financial Storytelling Toolkit

Imagine your collection of financial stories like a living, breathing garden. Some stories will bloom beautifully, capturing clients' imagination and illuminating complex ideas. Others might wither, failing to take root in the fertile ground of understanding.

Every client interaction is an opportunity for refinement. Pay attention to those magical moments when a story truly connects - when you see that spark of understanding light up in someone's eyes. What made that particular analogy work? Was it its simplicity? Its emotional resonance? The way it connected to a universal experience.

Start keeping a storytelling journal. After each client meeting, take a moment to reflect. Which analogies landed perfectly? Where did clients seem confused? Track these insights like a gardener notes the growth and challenges of different plants.

The Art of Analogy Development

Becoming a master financial storyteller is like developing any sophisticated skill. It requires practice, patience, and a willingness to be vulnerable. Choose five financial terms that consistently puzzle your clients. Challenge yourself to create multiple analogies for each.

Test these stories with people completely unfamiliar with financial concepts. Your partner, a friend, a family member - someone who knows nothing about investment strategies. Watch their facial expressions carefully. Listen to how they explain the concept back to you. If they can articulate the idea clearly, you've created a powerful narrative.

The Power of Perspective: Transforming Investment Narratives - The Language of Ownership

The words we choose when discussing investments with clients have profound implications. Consider this critical distinction in how we frame the very act of investing:

The Dinner Party: A Story About Perspective

James had been a financial adviser for fifteen years, but tonight he wasn't at work. He was at his neighbour's dinner party, enjoying a glass of wine and the pleasant buzz of conversation around the dining table.

"So, James," asked Sandra, his host's sister who was visiting from out of town, "what do you do for a living?"

"I'm a financial adviser," he replied, bracing himself for the usual reaction.

"Oh, how interesting!" Sandra smiled. "May I ask how do you invest your own money?"

James felt the other guests' attention shift to him. In the momentary silence, he considered his options. He could give his standard, brief answer, and move the conversation along, or he could take this opportunity to share something more meaningful.

"I invest in the stock market," he said simply, pausing to take a sip of wine.

Sandra's eyebrows shot up. "Wow, isn't that risky? Especially with everything going on in the world right now?"

James smiled slightly. "You know, there's always 'something going on in the world.' Always has been, always will be. Today's alarming headlines become tomorrow's footnotes or just another data point on a long-term chart. What feels like a crisis in the moment typically fades into statistical background noise over time."

Several other guests nodded in agreement. Thomas, a schoolteacher sitting across the table, added, "I've always been too nervous to put my money there. It seems like gambling to me."

James nodded, having heard these reactions countless times before. "That's what many people think," he agreed. "But let me share a different perspective."

He set down his glass and leaned forward slightly. "What if I told you that I invest at very low cost in thousands of the most innovative and profitable businesses in the world? I'm talking about companies that everyone we've ever known uses every day of their lives, whether they like all of them or not."

The table grew quiet as James continued.

"Think about it. When you woke up this morning, you probably checked your phone - made by one of the companies I own a small piece of. You brushed your teeth with toothpaste made by another company in my portfolio. You drove to work in a car manufactured by yet another, on roads built with equipment from even more companies I partially own. Virtually everyone we know probably uses about 20 companies a day without ever thinking about it. The phone network connecting your calls, the energy company heating your home, the brand of toiletries in your bathroom, the bank processing your transactions, the petrol in your car, the supermarket where you buy your groceries, the pharmaceutical company that made your prescription medicine—all of these are businesses that solve real problems for real people.

Take a walk down Oxford Street in London, and what do you see? Shops with customers buying clothes, people sipping coffee, tourists checking into hotels, delivery vans dropping off packages. Each of these represents real businesses selling real products and services to real people, generating real profits, 24 hours a day, all around the globe. That's not some abstract ticker symbol scrolling across a screen—that's what the stock market actually is.

And low-cost index tracking funds contain literally thousands of these great businesses from all around the world. Investors own a small piece of each and every one of them. Consider that the people running these businesses are smart, driven individuals constantly innovating and looking for ways to work around problems and maximise profits every step of the way. As part owners and investors, we benefit from these profits—providing we take a long-term view, remain patient, and stick to our plan through thick and thin.

Some worry that markets can't keep improving, that the good times must end. But as British historian Thomas Babington Macaulay wisely asked, 'On what principle is it that, when we see nothing but improvement behind us, we are to expect nothing but deterioration before us?' Throughout history, human innovation has consistently overcome challenges and created prosperity. Our job as investors is simply to participate in that remarkable journey."

When inexperienced investors see markets reach new all-time highs, they often believe the only direction left is down. Yet consider what these same investors would have been saying 10, 20, or 30 years ago—and look where markets stand today. Each generation faces this same psychological hurdle, seeing the summit as unsurpassable, yet markets have consistently climbed higher mountains over time. This pattern of doubt followed by growth has repeated throughout financial history, rewarding those with the patience and perspective to stay invested through cycles of uncertainty."

Thomas was now listening intently. "I never thought about it that way."

"The coffee you drank, the medication your daughter takes, the streaming service you watched last night, the grocery store where you shop - I own small pieces of all these businesses," James explained. "And as their owner, I partake in their profits when they do well, which, over the long term, the best ones tend to do."

Sandra tilted her head. "But what about when the market crashes? Doesn't that keep you up at night?"

James smiled. "Think of it this way: If you owned a successful local bakery, would you panic and sell it if someone offered you 30% less than its value today? Especially if the bakery's sales and profits continued to grow. Of course not. You'd recognise that the offer price doesn't reflect the true value of your business."

"The market goes up and down, certainly. But I'm not just buying abstract ticker symbols or playing a casino game. I'm buying ownership in real businesses that make real products, employ real people, and generate real profits. Over time, those businesses - at least the great ones - tend to become more valuable, not less."

By now, everyone at the table was engaged in the conversation. Even Mark, who had been checking his phone throughout dinner, was paying full attention.

"So, when someone asks me how I invest my money," James concluded, "I could simply say 'I invest in the stock market' and leave it at that. Or I could explain that I own small pieces of thousands of the world's greatest businesses that we all rely on every day. It's exactly the same thing - just viewed through a different lens."

After dinner, Thomas approached James privately. "You know, I've had some money sitting in a savings account for years earning almost nothing. The way you explained investing tonight - it actually makes sense to me now. I've always seen the stock market as this mysterious, dangerous thing. But owning parts of real businesses? That I can understand."

James smiled. "It's all about perspective. The facts haven't changed, just how we look at them."

Two weeks later, Thomas became James's newest client.

Adviser Reflection:

The story we tell matters deeply - both to our clients and to ourselves. When we frame investing as "buying the market," we invoke images of volatility, risk, and gambling. But when we frame it as "owning great businesses," we evoke stability, growth, and participation in the real economy.

Both descriptions are factually accurate, but they create vastly different emotional responses. By shifting our language from abstract financial concepts to concrete, real-world businesses that touch our clients' daily lives, we help them see investing not as speculation but as ownership - a profound shift that can transform their entire relationship with money and markets.

Addressing the "Crash and Lose Everything" Myth

Perhaps the most persistent and damaging investment misconception is the belief that market crashes mean investors will "lose all their money." This story provides a powerful framework for putting market volatility in proper perspective.

The End of Everything: A Story About Market Crash Fears

Sarah was visibly nervous as she sat across from Michael, her financial adviser. She had come in after the market had dropped 12% in a week, and the financial news channels were full of dire predictions and dramatic graphics with downward-pointing red arrows.

"I just don't know, Michael," she said, clutching her portfolio statement. "I keep thinking about my neighbour who lost everything in 2008. What if this is the big one? What if I lose all my money?"

Michael nodded sympathetically. He'd had this conversation many times before.

"Sarah, may I share something with you? It might help put things in perspective."

She nodded, still gripping the statement tightly.

"Imagine we're having coffee at your favourite café tomorrow morning," Michael began. "We're enjoying our conversation when suddenly we notice everyone outside is looking up at the sky. We step outside and see a massive asteroid hurtling toward Earth."

Sarah looked confused by this unexpected turn in the conversation.

"Or imagine instead," Michael continued, "that we turn on the news and discover that nuclear missiles have been launched by countries around the world, and impact is imminent."

"These are pretty dark scenarios, Michael," Sarah said with a nervous laugh. "How exactly is this supposed to make me feel better?"

Michael smiled. "Bear with me. In either of those scenarios, what would happen to your investment portfolio?"

"It would be wiped out, I suppose."

"Exactly. And would that be your primary concern at that moment?"

Sarah thought for a moment. "No... I'd be worried about my family, finding safety... basic survival."

"Precisely," Michael said. "Here's my point: There are really only two scenarios where you could lose literally every penny of your diversified investment. One is global thermonuclear war, and the other is a civilisation-ending asteroid strike. And in either case, as you just noted, money would be the least of your concerns."

He pulled out a sheet of paper. "For you to lose everything in your portfolio, every single one of these companies would need to simultaneously go bankrupt and never return."

He started pointing to familiar names on her investment holdings. "That means no more Apple, Google, or Microsoft. No more banks or payment systems. No more energy companies or utilities. No more food producers or retailers. No more pharmaceutical companies developing medications. No airlines, no hotels, no entertainment. Nothing."

Sarah was listening intently now.

"A market crash doesn't mean these companies cease to exist," Michael explained. "It means their share prices have dropped, often temporarily. People are still buying groceries, filling prescriptions, using electricity, and buying goods online during a market downturn. These businesses continue operating, generating revenue, and in many cases, still turning a profit."

Michael pulled out a historical chart of the market. "Look at every major crash in history—1929, 1987, 2000, 2008, 2020. In every case, the market eventually recovered and went on to new highs. Why? Because human innovation continues, populations grow, and businesses adapt."

"But my neighbour—" Sarah started.

"Let me guess," Michael interrupted gently. "Your neighbour who 'lost everything' in 2008 probably sold at the bottom of the market out of fear, turning a temporary paper loss into a permanent one. Or perhaps they had all their money concentrated in a few financial stocks rather than being globally diversified and were paying extortionate management fees. They didn't lose everything because the market crashed—they lost because of how they responded to the crash or how they were positioned before it."

Sarah was quiet, considering this.

"Here's another way to think about it," Michael said. "When the market drops 20%, it doesn't mean 20% of all businesses have disappeared. It means that, collectively, investors are valuing these ongoing businesses at 20% less than they did before. But the underlying companies—their workers, their factories, their intellectual property, their customer relationships—they're all still there, still functioning."

"So, what should I do during a crash?" Sarah asked, her grip on the statement finally loosening.

"First, remember that market crashes, while uncomfortable, are normal and expected parts of investing. Second, ensure you're properly diversified and invested according to your time horizon. And third, consider what a crash really means—it's essentially a sale on ownership of great businesses."

Michael leaned forward. "The only scenario in which diversified, long-term investors truly lose everything is one where money no longer matters anyway. Barring asteroids or nuclear war, businesses will continue to operate, adapt, and eventually thrive again."

Sarah started to get up, then hesitated. "One more thing, Michael. The news said the market crashed 20%. Does that mean my portfolio is down 20%?"

Michael smiled. "That's another important point. Let me explain something the headlines never mention."

He pulled out Sarah's investment summary. "Look at your portfolio. You're not 100% invested in stocks. You have a balanced portfolio—approximately 50% in stocks and 50% in bonds."

"How does that help?" Sarah asked.

"Well, when the news reports 'the market crashed 20%,' they're typically only talking about stocks—those ownership shares in great businesses we discussed. But bonds—which represent loans to governments and companies—often behave differently during market turbulence."

Michael drew a simple diagram on a notepad. "Let's say you have £100,000 invested. With your 50/50 split, that's £50,000 in stocks and £50,000 in bonds. If stocks drop 20%, your stock portion would be down to £40,000—a £10,000 temporary loss."

"But here's what the alarming headlines miss: bonds typically don't fall alongside stocks—they often move in the opposite direction or stay relatively stable. So, while your stocks might be down 20%, your bonds might be flat or even up a bit."

"So, my total portfolio wouldn't be down 20%?" Sarah asked.

"Exactly. In this scenario, your overall portfolio might only be down around 10%—half of what the scary headlines suggest. And that's a temporary decline, not a permanent loss unless you sell."

Michael closed the notepad. "The financial media rarely provides this context. 'Market Crashes 20%!' gets more clicks than 'Balanced Investors Might Experience Half the Volatility of All-Stock Portfolios.'"

"It's like weather reporting," he continued. "Imagine if the weather forecast only reported the day's low temperature without mentioning the high. You'd get a very distorted picture of what to expect."

Sarah nodded. "I never thought about it that way."

"That's why working with an adviser who can put these events in perspective is so important. The media's job is to attract attention. My job is to help you make sense of what's really happening and prevent panic decisions you might regret later."

As Sarah left the office, she felt a weight lift from her shoulders. The market hadn't changed, but her perspective had. And sometimes, that makes all the difference.

Adviser Reflection:

Many clients equate market crashes with total, permanent loss—an understandable fear, but one based on a fundamental misunderstanding of what the market is. By helping clients understand that a diversified portfolio can only be completely destroyed in scenarios where money becomes irrelevant, we help them contextualise market downturns appropriately.

This story addresses two persistent and damaging myths in investing: that market crashes equal "losing everything" and that headline percentage drops directly translate to their portfolio. By using the vivid imagery of truly apocalyptic scenarios versus the reality of what companies do during downturns, and by explaining the crucial distinction between stocks and bonds, advisers can help clients maintain perspective when markets inevitably decline.

Remember that most clients aren't afraid of volatility itself—they're afraid of what they think volatility means: permanent loss and financial ruin. Additionally, they often don't understand how asset allocation softens the impact of market volatility. By reframing market crashes as temporary repricing events rather than extinction events, and by explaining how diversification across asset classes provides a buffer against volatility, we help clients develop the emotional resilience needed for long-term investing success.

The financial media rarely provides these vital contexts, preferring attention-grabbing headlines to educational content. This is precisely why the art of storytelling is so crucial for financial advisers—it allows us to transform abstract concepts into understandable, memorable lessons that clients can hold onto when fear threatens to override reason.

Practical Application: Developing Your Own Investment Narratives

The stories above demonstrate the power of perspective in helping clients understand complex investment concepts. Below are some practical exercises to help you develop your own compelling investment narratives:

Exercise 1: Reframing Investment Concepts

Take these common investment terms and reframe them using more tangible, ownership-based language:

Traditional Term	Ownership-Based Reframing
Stock Market	Collection of businesses
Stock	Partial business ownership
Portfolio	Your business collection
Dividend	Your share of profits
Market Volatility	Changing business valuations
Diversification	Owning various businesses

Exercise 2: Creating Your Own Market Crash Story

Develop your own story addressing market crash fears by:

1. Identifying a specific client fear or misconception
2. Creating a relatable scenario or analogy
3. Building a narrative that transforms understanding
4. Practising delivery with colleagues for feedback

Exercise 3: Asset Allocation Visual Tools

Create simple visual aids to show clients how asset allocation works during market turbulence:

1. Develop a basic pie chart showing portfolio allocations
2. Create before/after illustrations of market movements
3. Design a "portfolio weather forecast" tool showing how different assets respond to market conditions

Remember that storytelling is about making abstract concepts tangible and relatable. By helping clients see investments as ownership in real businesses rather than abstract market movements, you provide the perspective needed for sound, long-term financial decision-making.

Conclusion: The Art of Financial Translation

Simplifying financial concepts isn't about dumbing down information. It's about lifting people up - helping them see beyond numbers to the real-world possibilities those numbers represent.

By breaking down intimidating terms, crafting relatable analogies, and testing our metaphors with genuine human insight, we transform complex ideas into practical wisdom. The magic happens when clients not only understand the advice but feel empowered by it.

In our next chapter, we'll dive deeper into the heart of financial storytelling. We'll explore how authenticity and personal experiences can transform a transactional interaction into a meaningful dialogue of possibility.

Your true role is to be a translator of dreams, a navigator of financial landscapes, and a trusted guide who helps people reimagine their relationship with money. It's about showing clients that their financial journey isn't just about numbers - it's about the life they want to create.

TEN KEY TAKEAWAYS

1. Simplifying complex financial concepts through stories doesn't mean dumbing down information—it means transforming abstract ideas into relatable narratives that empower clients and change their perspective on investing.

2. Reframing how we describe investments (from "buying the stock market" to "owning pieces of great businesses") can completely transform how clients perceive risk and opportunity, making the same information feel either threatening or empowering.

3. Market volatility becomes less frightening when placed in proper context through effective analogies—whether comparing it to a rollercoaster ride, turbulence on a flight, or explaining that total loss would require apocalyptic scenarios.

4. The stock market is the only store where people run away during sales—helping clients see market downturns as discount opportunities rather than threats creates a fundamental shift in their investment behaviour.

5. Visual and narrative tools help clients understand that market headlines rarely reflect their actual portfolio experience—showing how diversification across stocks and bonds creates resilience that sensationalist media never explains.

6. Financial decisions are deeply emotional, not just numerical, which is why stories that address both logical understanding and emotional perspective are essential for helping clients make sound decisions during challenging market conditions.

7. Analogies based on everyday experiences (shopping trolleys, house sales, cooking) make complex financial concepts instantly relatable, allowing clients to connect new knowledge to familiar activities.

8. Exponential concepts like compound interest are best explained through surprising visuals, like the folded paper example, which demonstrates how small consistent actions can lead to extraordinary results over time.
9. Effective financial communication focuses on the ultimate benefits and experiences that financial tools enable, rather than the tools themselves—clients don't dream about pensions, but about what those pensions make possible.
10. The financial adviser's most powerful role is as a perspective-shifter, helping clients see beyond short-term market movements to understand the fundamental principles that lead to long-term financial success.

CHAPTER 7

Building Trust Through Authentic Storytelling

---◇---

*"Honesty and transparency make you vulnerable.
Be honest and transparent anyway."*
—Mother Teresa

The best stories are the honest ones. In financial advising, trust is paramount, and one of the most powerful ways to build that trust is through authentic storytelling. Sharing your own financial experiences—mistakes and all—helps humanise you. It allows clients to see you not only as an adviser but as someone who has faced the same financial challenges, made decisions, learned from them, and ultimately found a path to success.

When you reveal a part of your journey, clients can connect with you on a personal level. It transforms you from a distant expert into a relatable guide, someone who's "walked the walk." This transparency fosters a deeper relationship and reassures clients that they're not alone in their financial concerns.

The Importance of Authenticity in Your Narratives

Authenticity is the foundation of any trust-based relationship. In storytelling, it's the difference between a story that resonates and one that feels rehearsed. Clients appreciate honesty and transparency, and authentic stories help bridge the gap between their own experiences and the advice you're offering. An authentic story doesn't shy away from showing vulnerability; in fact, sharing moments of uncertainty or regret makes your story more powerful.

When crafting authentic narratives, consider these principles:

1. **Be Genuine and Avoid Sugar-Coating:** Authentic stories include both the highs and the lows. Sharing a success story can be inspiring but revealing the mistakes you made along the way can make your story even more impactful. For example, instead of only discussing a successful investment, you could share a time when you misjudged the market or made an emotional decision, showing how you grew from the experience.

2. **Relate Personally:** Choose stories that connect with your client's circumstances. If you're advising a young professional starting their investment journey, share stories about your own beginnings, including the anxieties and uncertainties you faced. If you're working with someone near retirement, discuss the discipline needed to avoid impulsive decisions during market volatility.

3. **Show Your Values Through Stories:** Each story should reflect your core values as an adviser. If one of your values is long-term discipline, tell stories that highlight the importance of patience. If you prioritise client education, share stories about learning from your own mistakes or seeking guidance from mentors. Authenticity isn't just about honesty; it's about consistency in your message.

Consider this example of an authentic narrative:

"When I first started investing, I was convinced I could time the market perfectly. I pulled my money out during the 2008 financial crisis, thinking I'd reinvest when things 'settled down'. That moment never came—I missed the recovery and had to rebuild my strategy from scratch. That experience taught me the value of staying invested for the long term, a principle I now share with all my clients. It wasn't an easy lesson, but it shaped how I approach investing today."

This story demonstrates vulnerability, shares a genuine mistake, and connects to a valuable financial principle. By embedding authenticity in your stories, you foster a sense of trust that goes beyond data or financial analysis, positioning yourself as a guide who truly understands and empathises with clients' concerns.

Understanding What Clients Truly Value: Revealed vs Stated Preferences

One of the most valuable insights for financial advisers comes from understanding the difference between what clients say they want and what their actions reveal about their true preferences. This distinction is crucial for building authentic relationships and crafting stories that genuinely resonate.

Stated Preference: What clients say they want, often influenced by external factors like social expectations, media, or personal aspirations. For example, a client might claim they are comfortable with market volatility as long as it leads to higher long-term returns.

Revealed Preference: What a client's actual behaviour demonstrates. That same client who claimed to be comfortable with risk might panic and want to sell at the first sign of a market downturn.

Clients are not always aware of this gap themselves. They might genuinely believe they are long-term investors, but when faced with uncertainty, their emotions take over. The key to great financial advising is helping them reconcile their stated preferences with their revealed ones—without making them feel defensive or exposed.

How Storytelling Bridges This Gap

Instead of challenging a client's stated beliefs directly, storytelling allows them to see themselves in the experiences of others, prompting self-reflection in a more subtle and engaging way.

Revealing True Risk Tolerance

A client might say, "I understand that markets go up and down, and I won't panic when there's a downturn." But in reality, when the market drops, they may feel anxious and want to sell.

Rather than pointing out this contradiction directly, an adviser could tell a story:

The heavyweight boxer Mike Tyson famously said, "Everyone has a plan until they get punched in the mouth." What Tyson said is similar to the old saying, "No plan survives first contact with the enemy."

I'm reminded of this wisdom when thinking about investment risk. "I once worked with an investor who, like you, believed they could handle market volatility. But when 2008 hit—when they got 'punched in the mouth' by the market—they felt the urge to sell everything. Instead of reacting emotionally, we revisited their long-term plan. They stayed the course, and today, their portfolio is stronger than ever. That moment of hesitation turned into one of the best financial decisions they ever made."

This allows the client to reflect: Would I have done the same in that situation? Without feeling judged, they begin to recognise their true feelings about risk.

Identifying What Truly Matters

A client may state that they want the highest returns possible, but in reality, their revealed preference might be peace of mind and financial security.

A story that highlights this distinction might be:

"One of my clients was initially focused solely on maximising returns, often comparing his portfolio to market indices. During our review meetings, he'd express disappointment if his returns weren't matching the top performers. Then the pandemic hit. While his diversified portfolio dipped, it recovered steadily without the extreme volatility of the indices he'd been comparing himself to. In our next meeting, he admitted that what he truly valued wasn't outperforming the market—it was knowing he could sleep soundly despite market turmoil, confident his financial future remained secure."

By sharing stories that reveal this gap between stated and revealed preferences, you help clients develop greater self-awareness, leading to more authentic financial conversations and ultimately, better aligned financial plans.

Sharing Personal Experiences to Build Credibility

Personal experiences add credibility to your advice. When clients see that you've faced the same hurdles, they're more likely to believe in the strategies you recommend. Sharing stories about your own experiences brings a level of transparency that can make even complex concepts feel achievable.

Here's a complete example of a personal experience narrative you could use that builds credibility:

"Ten years into my career as a financial adviser, I faced a personal financial dilemma that tested everything I had been advising clients to do. My daughter had been accepted to university, and simultaneously, the property market was booming. I had the opportunity to either use my savings for a buy-to-let investment that promised significant returns or set that money aside for my daughter's education.

The investment property seemed like the better financial choice on paper. The projected returns were impressive, and property felt tangible and secure. But I kept thinking about what I always told my clients: 'Align your financial decisions with your core values.' While calculating potential returns, I realised I was letting short-term opportunity overshadow my long-term priorities.

I chose to fund my daughter's education, foregoing the property investment. Three years later, when the property market took an unexpected downturn, that decision proved financially prudent as well. But more importantly, it reinforced for me that financial decisions should reflect what we truly value, not just what might generate the highest return."

This kind of detailed personal story demonstrates that you've faced real financial crossroads, applied your own advice, and experienced both the challenges and benefits of making values-based decisions.

Other powerful personal experiences to share might include:

An Experience of Market Volatility

If clients are nervous about a volatile market, you might share a story from your early investment days when you experienced a significant market downturn. You could discuss the temptation to sell and how choosing to stay invested ultimately led to growth.

An Emotional Investing Lesson

Talk about a time when an emotional decision led to a mistake. Perhaps you were tempted to buy into a hot stock tip, only to watch it underperform. By admitting to your own moment of impulsivity, you illustrate that mistakes are normal and that learning from them is part of becoming a successful investor.

The Long Journey to Financial Goals

Many clients worry that their goals are too distant to achieve. Sharing a personal story about setting small, achievable milestones on your path to financial success can inspire them to take similar steps. For instance, if you steadily invested over many years to build a retirement fund, share how each small action compounded over time.

These personal stories bring a layer of realism and credibility to your advice, making clients feel more comfortable and confident in their financial journey. Here's another simple but powerful analogy I often use to help clients understand how short-term emotions can leave a permanent mark on long-term financial plans.

The Tattoo You Chose at 18

"Mike, I'm thinking about making a few changes to my portfolio," a client once told me during a volatile market period. "Maybe I should move into something that's performing better right now?"

I smiled, recognising that moment of uncertainty we all face. "Can I share something with you? It might help put things in perspective."

He nodded, and I continued, "Imagine you're 18 years old again. You're in a tattoo parlour with friends. You're absolutely convinced you'll love whatever design you pick forever. You choose the name of your favourite band—the one you're obsessed with right now—and have it prominently inked across your arm."

I paused, acknowledging the connection forming between us. "But five years later, the band has split up, the music sounds dated, and your life has moved on. What felt right at the time now feels permanent in all the wrong ways."

He chuckled, seeing where this was going.

"That's what making emotional financial decisions is like," I explained. "It feels urgent in the moment. It feels like the right choice. But these reactive decisions can leave a permanent mark on your long-term financial wellbeing."

I leaned in slightly. "When we let temporary emotions—market headlines, recent winners, short-term trends—drive permanent decisions, we risk tattooing mistakes onto our financial future."

He nodded thoughtfully.

"The real skill," I said, "is building a plan that reflects your enduring values and life goals, not your short-term feelings—and then having the patience to let it work. It might feel uncomfortable to stick with our strategy when everything around us is changing, but that discomfort is often the price of long-term success."

Empathy Mapping: Understanding the Emotional Landscape of Financial Decision-Making

Beyond traditional client profiling lies a deeper understanding of the emotional terrain that shapes financial choices. Empathy mapping is a powerful tool that goes beneath surface-level interactions, revealing the complex emotional and psychological drivers that truly influence financial decisions.

The Empathy Mapping Framework

A comprehensive empathy map for financial clients explores four critical dimensions:

1. **Says:**
   - Explicit financial concerns voiced by the client
   - Surface-level statements about money and goals
   - Verbalised fears and aspirations
2. **Thinks:**
   - Underlying financial anxieties
   - Unspoken concerns and internal dialogues
   - Hidden motivations and silent fears
3. **Feels:**
   - Emotional relationship with money
   - Deeper emotional responses to financial concepts
   - Psychological barriers to financial decision-making
4. **Does:**
   - Actual financial behaviours
   - Patterns of action (or inaction)
   - Disconnect between stated intentions and actual choices

Practical Application: The Emotional Financial Excavation

Let's look at a practical example of empathy mapping in action:

Client Profile: James, 45, Professional

Says: "I want to be more aggressive with my investments. I've been too conservative for too long."

Thinks: "What if I make a mistake? My colleagues seem to be doing better than me. I should have started investing earlier."

Feels: Anxiety about missing out, fear of making wrong decisions, guilt about past inaction, competitive with peers.

Does: Researches investments extensively but rarely acts, keeps significant cash in low-interest accounts, frequently changes his mind about investment strategies.

With this empathy map, you can craft stories specifically designed to address James's emotional landscape:

"I once worked with a client who, like you, felt he'd been too cautious with his investments. Every time he heard colleagues discussing their investment 'wins,' he felt he was falling behind. What he didn't hear were their losses—the risks that hadn't paid off. Together, we created a strategy that was more growth-oriented than his previous approach but still aligned with his true risk tolerance. Importantly, we established clear criteria for investment decisions, which freed him from the cycle of research paralysis and helped him act with confidence rather than anxiety."

This story addresses the gap between what James says he wants (more aggressive investments) and what his behaviour reveals (anxiety about making investment decisions). It acknowledges his competitive feelings without judgment and offers a pathway that respects both his stated goal and his emotional reality.

Techniques for Emotional Financial Mapping

1. Deep Listening Strategies

- Move beyond surface-level conversations
- Ask probing, non-judgmental questions
- Create a safe space for emotional vulnerability

2. Narrative Deconstruction

- Explore the origin of financial beliefs
- Identify emotional blocks to financial progress

- Help clients rewrite their financial narratives

Common Unspoken Financial Fears

Most clients will never explicitly state their deepest financial fears, but these often include:

- Fear of poverty
- Feeling of financial inadequacy
- Anxiety about future financial security
- Guilt about past financial mistakes
- Fear of making wrong decisions

By understanding these unspoken fears, you can craft stories that subtly address them, creating a sense of recognition and relief for clients who may have felt their concerns were unique or shameful.

Empathy is the bridge between financial data and human experience. Cross it with care, curiosity, and profound respect.

Addressing Common Client Concerns Through Stories

Clients come to you with a variety of concerns, from worries about market performance to fears about running out of money in retirement. By addressing these concerns through stories, you create a safe space for clients to feel seen and understood. Stories allow you to tackle sensitive topics without overwhelming clients with data alone.

Market Volatility and Patience

If a client is worried about market ups and downs, tell a story about a past client or personal experience where patience paid off:

"During the 2020 market crash, I worked with a couple who had just retired. As their portfolio dropped by nearly 30%, they were understandably terrified—their retirement dreams seemed to be evaporating before their eyes. We revisited their financial plan, confirming they had enough secure income to cover their essential expenses regardless of market conditions. Rather than selling in panic, they maintained their long-term investments. By early 2021, their portfolio had not only recovered but grown beyond its pre-crash value. Today, they often tell me that staying the course during that frightening time was the best financial decision they ever made, reinforcing that volatility is a natural part of investing that can be weathered with discipline."

Retirement Planning Anxiety

Many clients fear they won't have enough saved for retirement. You could share the story of someone who started later in life but achieved financial security:

"I remember working with a client who came to me at 52, worried she'd never be able to retire comfortably. She had only just started thinking seriously about retirement, having spent her earlier years focused on raising her children as a single mother. We created a plan that maximised her pension contributions, carefully allocated her investments based on her timeframe, and identified areas where she could reduce expenses. She committed to working until 68 and saving consistently. Today, at 70, she has a comfortable retirement income that supports both her basic needs and her passion for travel. Her story reminds me that while an early start is helpful, it's never too late to create a meaningful financial plan."

Avoiding "Get Rich Quick" Traps

Some clients may be tempted by the allure of quick gains, especially with trends in high-risk investments:

"A client once came to me excited about a cryptocurrency his colleague had invested in. The colleague had apparently doubled his money in just three months. My client was ready to move a significant portion of his retirement savings into this investment. Instead of dismissing his enthusiasm, I shared the story of another client who had invested heavily in technology stocks in the late 1990s, only to lose most of his investment when the dot-com bubble burst. We discussed how building wealth typically requires patience and a balanced strategy. Eventually, he decided to allocate just 5% of his portfolio to higher-risk investments, keeping the majority in a diversified, long-term strategy. When the cryptocurrency market crashed six months later, he thanked me for helping him maintain perspective."

Using storytelling to address these common concerns doesn't just answer clients' questions; it provides them with the assurance that their worries are both common and manageable. By sharing how others have successfully navigated similar situations, you offer a roadmap they can feel confident following.

Delivering Stories with Impact: Tone, Body Language, and Client Engagement

Great storytelling isn't just about the words you choose—it's also about how you deliver them. The way you communicate, both verbally and non-verbally, plays a crucial role in how clients perceive your message.

The Role of Body Language and Tone in Storytelling

Clients don't just listen to what you say—they interpret how you say it. Body language, facial expressions, and tone of voice all influence how authentic and trustworthy your story feels.

For Compassionate Stories: When sharing stories about financial hardship or difficult decisions, lean forward slightly, soften your voice, and maintain gentle eye contact. This physical positioning communicates empathy and creates a safe space for vulnerable conversations.

"When I'm discussing a client's fear of running out of money in retirement, I consciously slow my speech pattern and use a warmer tone. I've found that this combination of verbal and non-verbal cues helps diffuse the anxiety associated with this common fear, allowing us to address it constructively rather than emotionally."

For Inspirational Stories: When telling stories of financial success or resilience, use more animated gestures, varied vocal inflection, and energetic posture to convey enthusiasm and possibility.

"I worked with a couple who managed to pay off their mortgage in just seven years through disciplined saving and careful planning. When I share their story with other clients who have similar goals, I deliberately use an upbeat tone and more expressive hand gestures. This energy helps communicate not just the facts of their success but the feeling of accomplishment and freedom they experienced."

Remember that clients may not always recall your exact words, but they will remember how you made them feel. The right delivery transforms a good story into an unforgettable one.

Inviting Clients to Share Their Own Stories

Trust-building is not a one-way street. The best client conversations involve not just telling stories but inviting stories. When clients feel comfortable sharing their financial experiences—whether successes, struggles, or lessons learned—they become more engaged and invested in their own financial journey.

How to Prompt Clients to Share Stories

1. **Ask Reflective Questions:**

- "Have you ever made a financial decision that you later regretted? What did you learn from it?"
- "Who taught you the most about money growing up, and how has that shaped your approach to investing?"
- "If you could give financial advice to your younger self, what would it be?"

2. **Use Past Client Stories as a Mirror:**
   - "I had a client who hesitated to invest because of market uncertainty. Have you ever felt that way?"
   - "A couple I worked with worried about outliving their money—do you have the same concerns?"

3. **Acknowledge Their Experiences and Reframe Them:**
   - When a client shares their story, reflect it back to them and connect it to financial principles.
   - "That's a great insight—you're describing exactly why long-term discipline is so valuable."

When clients feel heard, they also feel understood. And when they connect their own experiences to the advice you're providing, they are more likely to trust and act on it. One way to encourage this is by asking, 'Given the facts as we understand them, if our roles were reversed and you were advising me, what would you suggest I do?' This simple shift in perspective helps them take ownership of the decision, reinforcing trust and confidence in the advice.

Overcoming Client Scepticism Through Storytelling

Not every client starts a financial conversation with an open mind. Some may be sceptical of advisers, fearing sales tactics, high fees, or conflicting interests. Others may have had poor past experiences, leading them to hesitate in trusting professional advice.

Using Storytelling to Build Trust with Sceptical Clients

Start with a story that acknowledges their doubts:

"When Sarah first came to see me, she made it clear that she wasn't sure financial advisers added any value. She'd been managing her own investments for years and had a previous experience with an adviser who seemed more interested in selling products than understanding her goals.

Rather than trying to convince her otherwise, I shared the story of another client with similar concerns who found value not in having someone else make decisions, but in having a thinking partner who could challenge assumptions and provide perspective during emotional market times. Six months later, Sarah told me that what she appreciated most was that I respected her intelligence and autonomy while still offering insights she hadn't considered."

This kind of story aligns with their fears but provides a resolution, helping the client see that they're not alone in their concerns.

Use Relatable Analogies

Many sceptical clients hesitate to delegate financial decisions because they feel they should "do it themselves."

A useful analogy might be:

"Think about elite athletes. Even Olympic gold medallists have coaches. Not because the coach is a better athlete, but because the coach provides perspective, expertise, and accountability that the athlete can't provide for themselves. Financial advising works similarly—my role isn't to take control away from you but to help you perform at your best financially."

This frames financial advice as a value-driven partnership rather than a sales pitch.

Practical Example: A Complete Client Storytelling Session

Let's bring together all these elements—authenticity, understanding revealed preferences, empathy mapping, addressing concerns, and effective delivery—in a complete client interaction:

Initial Client Statement: "I'm interested in investing, but I'm worried about market volatility. My parents lost a lot in 2008, and I don't want to make the same mistakes."

Adviser Response using Storytelling:

"Thank you for sharing that concern—it's one I hear often, especially from people who witnessed the impact of 2008 firsthand. Your caution is completely understandable.

You know, your experience reminds me of my own journey with investing. When I first started in financial services, I was incredibly risk averse. I'd seen how market crashes affected families, and I was determined to protect my clients from that kind of loss. I kept recommending the most conservative strategies possible.

But over time, I noticed something interesting. The clients who avoided all market exposure were actually falling behind on their long-term goals. They were avoiding one risk—market volatility—but unknowingly taking on another: the risk of their money not growing enough to support their future needs. They were avoiding the big risk of taking no risk.

I remember working with a couple, not unlike yourself, who were hesitant to invest after watching their parents struggle during the financial crisis. We started very conservatively, with just a small portion of their savings in the market. When the inevitable dips came, we used those as opportunities to discuss how temporary volatility differs from permanent loss. Each time the market recovered; their confidence grew.

Today, they have a diversified portfolio that's appropriate for their age and goals. What changed wasn't the market—it was their relationship with uncertainty. They came to understand that well-managed risk isn't something to fear but rather a necessary component of growth.

Would it be helpful if we explored what a balanced approach might look like for you? One that respects your concerns about volatility while still giving your money the opportunity to grow?"

In this example, the adviser:

- Acknowledged the client's concerns with empathy
- Shared an authentic personal story about evolving perspectives on risk
- Addressed the revealed preference (security) while gently challenging the stated concern (all market exposure is dangerous)
- Used a relevant client story to provide a potential path forward
- Delivered the message with a tone of respect and understanding
- Invited the client into the conversation rather than prescribing a solution

Conclusion: The Power of Authentic Storytelling

Authentic storytelling transforms the adviser-client relationship from a transactional exchange to a meaningful partnership built on trust and understanding. By sharing genuine experiences, recognising the emotional landscape of financial decisions, and delivering stories with impact, you create connections that data alone cannot achieve.

The most effective financial advisers are those who recognise that clients don't just want expertise—they want a guide who understands their journey, acknowledges their fears, and helps them navigate their financial future with confidence. Authentic storytelling is the bridge that connects your professional knowledge with your client's personal history and experience.

In the next chapter, we'll explore how to enhance client engagement by using visual storytelling techniques that make complex financial concepts more accessible and memorable, turning abstract ideas into tangible understanding.

EIGHT KEY TAKEAWAYS

1. Authentic storytelling builds trust by humanising you as an adviser, transforming you from a distant expert into a relatable guide who has faced similar financial challenges and learned from them.
2. The distinction between revealed and stated preferences is crucial. Clients may say they can handle market volatility (stated preference) but panic when markets drop (revealed preference), which storytelling can address indirectly.
3. Personal experience stories add credibility to your advice, demonstrating that you've applied your own principles in real-life situations, making complex concepts feel more achievable to clients.
4. Empathy mapping explores four critical dimensions (Says, Thinks, Feels, Does) to understand the emotional drivers behind financial decisions, allowing you to craft stories that address clients' unspoken fears.
5. Effective story delivery involves both what you say and how you say it—using appropriate body language, tone, and pacing to convey compassion for difficult topics or enthusiasm for inspirational ones.
6. Stories can effectively address common client concerns like market volatility, retirement planning anxiety, and investment temptations in a way that data alone cannot.
7. Inviting clients to share their own stories creates stronger engagement and helps them take ownership of their financial journey.
8. Strategic storytelling can help overcome scepticism in clients who may be distrustful of financial advisers based on past experiences.

CHAPTER 8

Engaging Your Audience: Techniques and Strategies

---◇---

> "The success of your presentation will be judged
> not by the knowledge you send but by what
> the listener receives."
> —*Lilly Walters*

A good story is like a good meal—you savour it, share it, and remember it.

The Tennis Match of Financial Storytelling

Picture a tennis match—not just any match, but a masterful dialogue of skill, strategy, and intuitive connection. Financial storytelling is remarkably similar. Just as a tennis player doesn't simply launch balls across the court, a financial adviser doesn't merely deliver information. Each interaction is a carefully choreographed exchange, a dynamic rally of understanding.

In tennis, a great player reads their opponent's stance, anticipates their next move, and responds with precision. Similarly, exceptional financial storytelling is about reading your client's emotional and intellectual landscape, anticipating their concerns, and responding with narratives that illuminate, engage, and transform.

Reading the Narrative Landscape

Just as a tennis player becomes attuned to the subtle nuances of the court, a financial storyteller develops an extraordinary sensitivity to client communication. Every furrow of the brow, every moment of hesitation, every glazed expression becomes a signal—an invitation to adjust your narrative approach.

Imagine a client whose body language suggests confusion during a technical explanation. Their slightly tilted head, the way their eyes drift, the nervous fidgeting—these are not obstacles, but opportunities. Much like a tennis player reading an opponent's positioning, you're gathering critical information about how to correct, how to explain, how to truly communicate.

The Serve: Capturing Attention

Every great tennis match begins with a powerful serve. In storytelling, this is your opening moment—the instant you capture a client's imagination. But a truly remarkable serve isn't about power; it's about strategic placement, about creating an unexpected angle that makes the listener lean in.

Consider how you might begin a narrative about long-term investing. Instead of dry statistics, you might say: "Financial journeys are like mountain expeditions. Some climbers rush ahead, chasing quick summits. Others understand that true progress is about consistent movement, strategic pauses, and understanding the entire landscape."

The Art of Conversational Transitions

In tennis, movement between shots is as crucial as the shots themselves. Narrative transitions require similar grace and intentionality. The language you use becomes a bridge, transforming technical information into compelling stories.

"This reminds me of a journey that might help explain..." A simple phrase that invites your client into a shared exploration. "Let me share an example that brings this to life..." These are not just words, but strategic invitations that turn monologues into dialogues.

The Rally: Interactive Storytelling

The heart of tennis is the rally—a back-and-forth exchange of extraordinary skill and intuition. Financial storytelling follows the same principle. Each story you share is an invitation to dialogue, not a monologue.

When you introduce a financial concept, create space for participation. "How does this resonate with your experience?" Translate complex ideas into familiar territories. For a client who loves gardening, investment diversification becomes about cultivating a garden with varied plants, each thriving in different conditions.

Strategic Shot Selection: Narrative Techniques

Just as a tennis player selects shots based on the court's conditions, a financial storyteller must choose narrative approaches with similar precision. The drop shot—an unexpected, gentle insight that requires the client to lean in. The lob—a broad, comprehensive view that provides context. The volley—quick, successive insights that build momentum and understanding.

Understanding Different Players

Different clients are like different tennis opponents. The analytical player requires data-driven narratives with clear logical progression. The intuitive strategist connects through broader life contexts and emotional resonance. The conservative defender needs reassurance and stories of stability. The bold challenger responds to narratives of opportunity and strategic risk-taking.

Psychological Positioning

Financial storytelling transcends mere information delivery. It's about creating a psychological space where clients feel understood, where complex concepts become accessible journeys of potential transformation.

When a client shares a financial concern, they're rarely just discussing money. They're revealing their hopes, fears, and deepest aspirations for security and possibility. Your narrative becomes a bridge, transforming abstract financial concepts into meaningful personal experiences.

Managing Unexpected Volleys

In tennis, the best players adapt instantly to unexpected shots. Similarly, client interruptions are not disruptions but opportunities for deeper connection. A client's mid-story question is an invitation to dive deeper. "Excellent observation—let me show you how this connects to the broader narrative we're exploring."

The Mental Game: Building Narrative Resilience

The most profound financial stories are not about perfect strategies, but about human capacity for adaptation and growth. They reveal financial journeys as continuous learning experiences, where challenges are opportunities for strategic reimagining.

Closing the Match: Crafting Memorable Conclusions

Like a tennis champion's final, decisive shot, the conclusion of your financial narrative is where impact truly crystallises. Your story's ending should be more than a mere summary—it must be a powerful distillation of insight that resonates long after the conversation ends.

Imagine each narrative conclusion as a strategic point in a championship match. You're not just ending a story; you're leaving an indelible mark on your client's financial understanding. The most memorable conclusions do more than inform—they inspire, challenge, and transform.

Effective endings might reframe the entire journey. "Today's challenges are tomorrow's opportunities" becomes more than a platitude—it's a strategic perspective. A conclusion that connects back to the client's deepest aspirations, that shows how today's decisions ripple into future possibilities, creates a lasting impact.

The Court of Communication: Physical Positioning

Your physical environment is as crucial as your narrative strategy. Consider your consulting space like a carefully prepared tennis court—every element matters.

Position yourself at a careful angle that allows natural, non-threatening eye contact. This isn't about confrontation, but connection. Your visual aids—whiteboards, tablets, charts—should be like well-placed tennis racquets. Close enough to be useful, but not so prominent that they distract from the human connection.

Ensure your client feels comfortable, free from external distractions. The physical space should feel like a collaborative arena, not an interrogation room. A carefully arranged environment communicates professionalism, openness, and partnership.

The Vocal Technique: Your Narrative Instrument

Your voice is as nuanced an instrument as a finely tuned tennis racquet. Each variation in tone, each strategic pause, can shift the entire dynamic of your narrative.

Begin with a slight pause—a moment of anticipation, like a player preparing to serve. This signals a transition, draws attention. When introducing critical concepts, lower your voice slightly. This isn't about volume, but intimacy. You're inviting the client into a confidential, shared exploration.

Slow your pace when setting up a story's landscape. Allow each word to breathe, to create mental imagery. Your tone should feel conversational, as if you're sharing insights with a trusted colleague over coffee, not delivering a formal presentation.

The conversational approach transforms your narrative from a monologue to a dialogue. You're not lecturing; you're exploring together. Each vocal shift is a strategic shot, designed to engage, to illuminate, to connect.

The Final Serve

Remember, in both tennis and financial storytelling, it's not about winning or losing. It's about the quality of the exchange, the mutual understanding, and the journey of growth you facilitate.

Your narrative is more than a collection of facts. It's a bridge between current understanding and future possibility. Each story you tell is an invitation—to learn, to grow, to see financial challenges not as obstacles, but as opportunities for strategic transformation.

The Federer Principle: Embracing Imperfection in Financial Storytelling

Roger Federer's profound wisdom extends far beyond the tennis court, offering a transformative perspective for financial advisers and their clients. In his 2024 Dartmouth commencement address, Federer revealed a staggering statistic: throughout his illustrious career, he won just 54% of the points in his 1,526 singles matches—despite winning nearly 80% of those matches.

This numerical revelation is a powerful metaphor for financial journeys. Success is not about perfection, but about resilience, perspective, and the ability to focus on the next point—or in our world, the next financial opportunity.

Federer taught us that the greatest skill is not avoiding challenges but becoming a master at overcoming them. In financial storytelling, this means helping clients understand that setbacks are not failures, but integral parts of their financial narrative. The most successful investors, like the most accomplished athletes, know that losing is not just inevitable—it's an essential part of growth.

Consider the energy we often waste dwelling on financial missteps. A missed investment opportunity, a market downturn, an unexpected expense—these moments can consume us with negative energy. Federer's wisdom cuts through this: negative energy is wasted energy. Instead, accept the moment. Feel the disappointment if you must. Then force a smile and move forward.

This is the essence of resilient financial storytelling. It's not about crafting narratives of uninterrupted success, but about creating stories of adaptability, of learning, of continuous movement. Just as Federer learned to not dwell on every lost point, we help our clients learn not to be paralysed by every financial challenge.

Your role as a financial storyteller is to be a coach, a guide who helps clients see beyond the immediate setback. Show them how each challenge is an opportunity to learn, to adjust, to grow. Help them understand that their financial journey is not measured by individual moments of loss, but by their ability to keep moving forward.

In the grand match of financial planning, perfection is not the goal. Resilience is. Growth is. The ability to face each point—each financial decision—with courage, wisdom, and an unwavering commitment to moving forward.

In the next chapter, we will explore how to communicate effectively across various media without losing the heart of the story. From social media snippets to in-depth webinars, understanding how to tailor storytelling for different platforms will help advisers connect with their audience in meaningful ways, no matter where or how they engage.

FIVE KEY TAKEAWAYS

1. Financial storytelling is like a tennis match—a dynamic, interactive exchange where you must read your client's emotional and intellectual responses and adapt your narrative approach accordingly.

2. The opening of your story (the "serve") needs strategic placement rather than just power, creating an unexpected angle that captures client attention and makes them lean in to learn more.

3. Physical positioning and environment matter—arrange your consulting space to allow natural eye contact, minimise distractions, and ensure your visual aids complement rather than dominate the human connection.

4. Your voice is a nuanced instrument in storytelling—strategic pauses, tone variations, and conversational pacing transform your narrative from a monologue into a dialogue that invites collaboration.

5. The "Federer Principle" reminds us that financial success, like tennis, isn't about perfection but resilience—winning just 54% of points can lead to winning 80% of matches, teaching clients that setbacks are not failures but essential parts of growth.

CHAPTER 9

Storytelling Across Different Media

"The medium is the message."
—Marshall McLuhan

Imagine standing in a room full of diverse individuals, each with a unique way of listening, learning, and understanding. This is precisely the challenge financial advisers face in the digital age. We're no longer confined to face-to-face meetings or traditional communication channels. Instead, we must become narrative chameleons, adapting our stories to multiple platforms while maintaining their essential truth.

Different media are like musical instruments, each with their own unique timbre and resonance. Social media plays like a punchy trumpet, quick and attention-grabbing. Newsletters become a rich cello, deep and informative. Video content dances like a vibrant violin, engaging multiple senses. Podcasts whisper like a gentle flute, building intimacy and trust. Webinars orchestrate a full ensemble, creating interactive, real-time connections.

The art of modern financial storytelling is about understanding these instruments and playing them with skill and intention.

Understanding Learning Styles: The Personal Connection

Every client processes information differently. Some are visual learners who need charts and graphs to make sense of abstract financial concepts. Others are verbal processors who thrive on in-depth conversations and narrative explanations. Some prefer written documentation they can study at their own pace, meticulously working through detailed reports.

Consider Sarah, a marketing executive who loves visual presentations. Hand her a text-heavy report, and her eyes glaze over. But show her a carefully crafted infographic demonstrating compound interest, and suddenly, complex financial principles become crystal clear. Conversely, her colleague James prefers deep, conversational exploration, asking probing questions and working through concepts verbally.

The most effective financial advisers are linguistic translators, capable of speaking multiple communication languages. They recognise that great advice isn't just about what is said, it's about how it is understood.

Social Media: The Art of Micro-Storytelling

Social media demands a different storytelling approach—think of it as financial poetry rather than prose. You have mere seconds to capture attention, to distil complex ideas into their most potent form. A compelling social media story might begin with an unexpected question: "What if the best investment strategy is doing absolutely nothing?" Or it might showcase a transformative client journey: "How one client turned £10,000 into £1,000,000 without losing sleep."

The key is brevity combined with emotional resonance. Pair your micro-story with a striking visual—perhaps a graph showing the power of long-term investing—and you've created a narrative that can stop a scrolling thumb in its tracks.

Newsletters and Blogs: The Narrative Deep Dive

If social media is a headline, newsletters and blogs are the long-form investigative piece. Here, you can explore complex concepts with nuance and depth. A blog post about diversification isn't just a technical explanation, it's a story of financial strategy, risk management, and client triumph.

Structure becomes crucial. Break your narrative into digestible sections. Use headings that guide the reader, like chapters in a book. "How Diversification Saved My Client During the 2008 Crash" might include sections exploring the challenge, the strategy, and the ultimate outcome.

Real-life, anonymised case studies become your most powerful tool. Imagine sharing how a client navigated the 2008 financial crisis by staying diversified, while others panicked. Their portfolio not only recovered but grew 40% within five years—a testament to strategic patience.

Video Content: Storytelling Beyond Words

Video storytelling transcends language. Your tone, body language, and visual cues become as important as the words themselves. Imagine explaining compound interest through an animated journey, showing how a small seed of investment grows into a magnificent financial tree.

Keep videos concise—one to three minutes is optimal. Focus on a single, powerful message. End with a clear, actionable invitation: "Want to discover how this strategy could transform your financial future? Let's have a conversation."

Podcasts: The Intimate Narrative Medium

Podcasts offer an extraordinary opportunity for deep, conversational storytelling. Here, you're not just sharing information, you're building a relationship. Invite guests who can share unique perspectives. Create episodes around compelling themes like "Overcoming Market Fear" or "The Power of Patience in Investing."

Encourage listener interaction. Ask them to share their own financial stories, creating a community of learning and shared experience.

The Nuanced Art of Live Storytelling

There's a magical difference between telling a story in an intimate conversation and commanding the attention of a live audience. Live storytelling is performance art, requiring a symphony of vocal technique, physical presence, and psychological connection.

Imagine standing in front of a room full of potential clients, your voice, an instrument capable of multiple registers. In one moment, you might drop to a hushed, intimate tone that draws listeners closer. In the next, you might raise your volume to emphasise a critical point, creating a moment of collective realisation. Your pacing becomes a narrative heartbeat, sometimes rapid with excitement, sometimes slow and deliberate to underscore significance.

Physical movement becomes part of your storytelling vocabulary. A step forward can signal intimacy; a gesture can illustrate a complex financial concept. When explaining market volatility, your hands might mimic the rises and falls of an investment graph. A raised eyebrow can communicate nuance; a knowing smile can build connection.

Audience participation transforms passive listening into active engagement. "Raise your hand if you've ever felt anxious about investing," you might say, creating an instant sense of shared experience. These moments break down barriers, turning a presentation into a collective journey.

Webinars and Live Presentations: Interactive Storytelling

Live storytelling is performance art. Begin with a powerful anecdote that sets the tone. Use visual aids—slides, graphs, short videos—to complement your narrative. Create moments of interaction, inviting questions and comments that transform your presentation from a monologue to a dialogue.

Measuring Your Storytelling's True Impact

How do we know our stories are truly resonating? In the digital age, engagement is our most valuable currency. Each platform offers unique metrics that reveal the heartbeat of our narrative.

On social media, likes and shares are more than vanity metrics—they're pulses of connection. A post about long-term investing that garners dozens of shares isn't just content; it's a conversation starter. Newsletters reveal their magic through open rates and time spent reading. Are clients devouring your words, or merely skimming?

Video content speaks through views and retention. A three-minute explainer on compound interest that keeps viewers watching until the end? That's a story that matters. Podcasts and webinars offer the most intimate measurement—direct feedback, personal stories shared in response to your narrative.

Transforming Stories into Meaningful Action

Great storytelling is a bridge, not a destination. Every narrative should carry your audience towards a meaningful next step. Your call to action is the bridge's final span, connecting insight to action.

Crafting the perfect call to action is an art form. It must be:

- Crystal clear in its invitation
- Aligned precisely with the story's message
- Urgent without feeling manipulative
- Personal enough to feel like a conversation, not a sales pitch

"Let's chart your financial future together, schedule a call today" isn't just an invitation. It's a promise of partnership, of possibility.

Consider the power of specificity. Instead of a generic "Contact us", imagine: "Curious how we helped Sarah turn uncertainty into financial confidence? Let's explore your unique path." Suddenly, it's not about a service, it's about a transformation.

Artificial Intelligence: The New Frontier of Financial Storytelling

Artificial Intelligence is not a replacement for human storytelling, it's a powerful amplifier of human creativity. In the world of financial communication, AI emerges as a sophisticated collaborator, offering unprecedented opportunities to craft more personalised, insightful, and impactful narratives.

Imagine AI as a highly intelligent research assistant, data interpreter, and creative partner. It doesn't write your story; it provides the insights, nuances, and context that make your storytelling more profound and precisely targeted.

Personalisation at Scale: AI can analyse vast amounts of client data to help you craft stories that speak directly to individual experiences. Where once personalisation was time-consuming, now it becomes both nuanced and efficient. A story about retirement planning can be subtly adjusted to resonate with a 35-

year-old tech professional versus a 55-year-old small business owner.

The most critical aspect of AI in storytelling is understanding its role as a tool, not a storyteller. Financial stories are deeply personal, requiring emotional intelligence, empathy, and nuanced understanding that AI cannot fully replicate.

Your unique experiences, your ability to read a client's emotional landscape, your capacity for genuine connection, these remain irreplaceable. AI can provide the scaffolding, but the soul of the story comes from you.

Practical applications range from content research to narrative refinement, helping you identify emerging trends, compile insights, and suggest more compelling ways to express complex financial concepts. But the human touch remains paramount—edit, refine, and ensure the story remains authentically yours.

The Boundless Potential of Your Financial Narrative

In an increasingly digital world, the fundamental power of storytelling remains unchanged. It's about connection, understanding, and transformation. By mastering the nuances of different media, you can ensure your financial stories resonate deeply, regardless of the platform.

As we stand at the intersection of technology and human connection, remember this: Your stories are more than words. They are bridges between fear and understanding, between uncertainty and confidence.

What story will you tell today? How will you transform a simple message into a journey of financial empowerment?

The next chapter of your client's financial story begins with your next word.

We've explored the art of crafting compelling narratives across various media—each platform offering unique opportunities to connect, educate, and inspire. But storytelling in financial advisory is more than just technique. It's about transformation. And what transforms a good story into a powerful narrative? Evidence. Real-world examples that breathe life into abstract concepts, turning promising theories into proven pathways.

This is where case studies become the cornerstone of impactful financial storytelling. While the techniques we've discussed provide the framework, case studies are the structural beams that support the entire narrative. They are living proof of the strategies, the analogies, and the principles we've explored. Where storytelling creates possibility, case studies demonstrate probability. They answer the critical question every client asks: "Can this really work for me?"

In the next chapter, we'll dive deep into the art of turning financial journeys into compelling narratives that don't just tell a story, they prove a point, inspire action, and transform understanding.

FIVE KEY TAKEAWAYS

1. Different media platforms require different storytelling approaches—social media demands brevity and emotional resonance, newsletters allow for deeper exploration, and video content engages multiple senses simultaneously.

2. Understanding various learning styles is crucial—visual learners need charts and graphics, verbal processors thrive on conversations, and others prefer written documentation they can study at their own pace.

3. Live storytelling requires mastering vocal techniques, physical presence and audience participation to create interactive experiences that transform presentations from monologues into dialogues.

4. Measuring storytelling impact varies by platform—from social media engagement to newsletter open rates, video retention metrics, and direct feedback from podcasts and webinars—each revealing how stories resonate.

5. Artificial Intelligence serves as an amplifier of human creativity rather than a replacement, helping to personalise stories at scale while the financial adviser remains the source of emotional intelligence and authentic connection.

CHAPTER 10

Case Studies and Practical Examples

―――――◇―――――

*"Example isn't another way to teach,
it is the only way to teach."*
—Albert Schweitzer

Stories are the bridges between concepts and action. Case studies anchor those bridges in reality.

Financial advice lives and breathes through real-world experiences. Abstract theories become meaningful only when they transform into tangible human journeys. Every number, every strategy, every financial principle finds its true purpose in the lived experiences of those who navigate economic challenges and opportunities.

Consider the profound difference between theoretical advice and a story that reveals how a strategy actually works. A spreadsheet might show potential returns, but a case study shows transformation. It's the difference between reading about swimming and watching someone navigate challenging waters with skill and confidence.

The true power of case studies lies in their ability to bridge understanding. They are more than simple narratives—they are living proof of financial possibilities. When a client hears how someone similar to them overcame a financial challenge, something remarkable happens. Doubt gives way to hope. Uncertainty transforms into confidence.

The Anatomy of Compelling Case Studies

Not every story becomes a powerful case study. The most effective narratives share critical characteristics that resonate deeply with clients. They must reflect genuine human experiences, showcase clear challenges, and demonstrate meaningful strategies and outcomes.

Consider the essential elements that make a case study truly impactful

Credibility emerges when clients see real-world evidence of financial strategies in action. It's not about presenting perfect scenarios but about showing authentic journeys of financial growth and challenge. Each case study becomes a testament to the possibility of financial transformation.

Relatability is the heart of effective storytelling. Clients do not want to hear about abstract success—they want to see themselves in the narrative. A powerful case study allows clients to imagine their own potential, to see their struggles reflected and their hopes validated.

Memorability comes from storytelling that engages both logic and emotion. When a financial journey is told with nuance, with human detail, it becomes more than information—it becomes an inspiration.

Selecting Narratives that Resonate

The most compelling case studies emerge from diverse experiences. A retirement planning story might show how a late saver achieved financial security through disciplined investing. A market volatility narrative could demonstrate how a client stayed invested during a downturn and reaped long-term rewards. A debt management journey might reveal how a young professional eliminated debt while simultaneously building savings.

Each narrative must be carefully curated. The goal is not to showcase perfection, but to illustrate growth, strategy, and human resilience.

Crafting the Narrative Arc

Every meaningful case study follows a classic storytelling structure: a clear beginning, a transformative middle, and a powerful conclusion.

The introduction reveals the initial challenge—the financial uncertainty, the seemingly insurmountable obstacle. It humanises the story, allowing other clients to see themselves in that moment of vulnerability.

The journey explores the strategy—the collaborative process of understanding, planning, and taking calculated steps. This is where financial advice becomes more than numbers. It becomes a partnership, a shared exploration of possibility.

The outcome demonstrates results, but more importantly, it reveals lessons. It's not just about the financial gain, but about the personal growth, the newfound confidence, the expanded understanding of what's financially possible.

Practical Narratives: Real Stories, Real Transformations

Let us explore three journeys that illustrate the profound impact of thoughtful financial guidance.

John's story begins with panic during a market downturn. Tempted to sell everything, he instead learned about market cycles, historical recoveries, and the importance of staying committed to long-term goals. Within two years, his portfolio not only recovered but grew by 25%. The key lesson: market declines are temporary, but strategic patience is permanent.

Sarah's journey started with fear—a common barrier to investing. By comparing investment to gardening, we reframed her understanding. "You won't see results overnight," we explained, "but with time and care, your investments will grow." Starting with a small, diversified portfolio, she gradually built confidence. Three years later, she was not just invested, but excited about her financial future.

Tom's narrative emerged later in life. An entrepreneur who realised retirement was approaching faster than anticipated, he needed a rapid, strategic approach. We created a tailored plan maximising contributions, leveraging tax-efficient accounts, and investing strategically. By 65, he had built a comfortable retirement fund that balanced growth and preservation.

Beyond Numbers: The Human Element

Case studies are more than mathematical demonstrations. They are stories of human potential, of overcoming financial fears, of transforming uncertainty into opportunity.

Visuals can enhance these narratives—charts showing portfolio growth, infographics illustrating strategic steps, before-and-after comparisons that make the journey tangible. But the most powerful visual is always the human story behind the numbers.

Personalisation is Key

Different clients require different narratives. Younger individuals might connect with stories about debt management and initial investing. Retirees seek reassurance through income planning and wealth preservation narratives. High-net-worth clients appreciate insights into tax efficiency and legacy planning.

The Ethical Dimension

With storytelling comes responsibility. Every case study must be crafted with integrity, anonymised to protect privacy, and shared with the genuine intention of education and inspiration.

Client testimonials, shared ethically and with permission, add authenticity. Hearing directly from those who have walked the path can be profoundly motivating.

Your Narrative Library

Begin collecting your stories. Each case study is a testament to financial possibility, a beacon of hope for those navigating complex economic landscapes.

Compile these narratives carefully. Update them regularly. Let them reflect the dynamic, human nature of financial journeys.

Stories have the power to transform abstract concepts into lived experiences. They bridge understanding, inspire action, and reveal the deeply human side of financial planning.

In our next chapter, we will explore the ethical considerations that must guide our storytelling, ensuring that every narrative we share reinforces trust, transparency, and genuine client care.

FIVE KEY TAKEAWAYS

1. Case studies transform abstract financial theories into tangible human journeys, serving as "living proof" of financial possibilities that bridge the gap between concepts and action.

2. Effective case studies share three critical characteristics: credibility (showing authentic financial strategies in action), relatability (allowing clients to see themselves in the narrative), and memorability (engaging both logic and emotion).

3. Every compelling case study follows a classic narrative arc: beginning (the financial challenge), middle (the strategy and collaborative process), and conclusion (outcomes and lessons learned).

4. The most powerful case studies focus on the human story behind the numbers, demonstrating not just financial gains but personal growth, newfound confidence, and expanded understanding of what's possible.

5. Personalisation is essential—different clients connect with different narratives, requiring advisers to maintain a diverse "narrative library" that addresses various life stages, financial situations, and client concerns.

CHAPTER 11

Ethics and Responsibility in Storytelling

"With great power comes great responsibility."
—Uncle Ben, Spider-Man

As financial advisers, we wield tremendous influence through our stories. The narratives we share can inspire clients to make life-changing decisions, help them navigate complex financial landscapes, and empower them to secure their futures. But this influence carries a profound ethical responsibility. When used thoughtfully, storytelling builds trust and understanding; when misused, it can mislead and manipulate. The difference lies in our —commitment to ethical principles that place our clients' interests at the heart of every story we tell.

In my years of working with advisers, I've observed that those who command the greatest respect are not necessarily those with the most impressive investment returns or the largest client base, but rather those who communicate with unwavering integrity. Their stories ring true because they are true—authentic reflections of financial realities, told with the genuine intention to guide and educate.

The Foundation of Ethical Storytelling

Ethical storytelling begins with integrity—a quality that cannot be faked or manufactured. Your clients entrust you with their financial wellbeing, and your stories should honour that trust through honesty, relevance, and transparency.

When I speak of integrity in storytelling, I'm referring to three essential principles that form the cornerstone of ethical financial communication:

Truthfulness is non-negotiable. Every story you share—whether about market trends, investment outcomes, or client experiences—must be factually accurate. This doesn't mean your stories can't be compelling or emotionally resonant; it simply means they must be grounded in reality. For instance, when highlighting how compound interest can grow wealth, use realistic return rates rather than exceptional ones that might create unrealistic expectations.

Transparency about your intentions transforms a good story into an ethical one. Before sharing a narrative, ask yourself: "Why am I telling this particular story? What am I hoping my client will understand or do as a result?" Then, make that intention clear. If you're sharing a story about market volatility to help a client understand the importance of staying invested during downturns, state this purpose explicitly: "I'd like to share a story that illustrates why patience during market uncertainty can be rewarding."

Relevance ensures that your stories serve your clients' specific needs. A story that perfectly motivated one client might fall flat or even mislead another with different circumstances, goals, or risk tolerance. Tailor your narratives to address the unique financial journey of each person sitting across from you.

Consider James, an adviser who works primarily with pre-retirees. When discussing retirement planning with a couple five years from retirement, he could share a generic story about the benefits of diversification. Instead, he chooses to tell them about another couple in a similar situation who had initially resisted rebalancing their portfolio, which had become heavily weighted toward technology stocks. When the sector experienced volatility, they faced a significant setback in their retirement timeline. This story resonates because it's directly relevant to their life stage and potential risks.

Avoiding Manipulative Storytelling

We've all encountered manipulative storytelling in our lives—the salesperson who focuses only on benefits while glossing over risks, the advertisement that plays on our deepest fears, or the investment opportunity that sounds too good to be true. As financial advisers, we have an ethical obligation to recognise and avoid these tactics, even when they might seem effective in the short term.

Manipulative storytelling often reveals itself through certain patterns. Learning to recognise these patterns in your own communication is the first step toward more ethical practice:

Fear-based narratives that overemphasise worst-case scenarios can pressure clients into making hasty decisions. Instead of telling a client, "Without this insurance product, your family could be destitute if you die," consider a more balanced approach: "Let me share how appropriate life insurance has provided peace of mind for clients in similar family situations, while explaining how we determine the right level of coverage based on your specific needs."

Product-focused stories that seem designed primarily to sell rather than educate should raise a red flag. When your stories consistently lead to the same product recommendation regardless of the client's situation, it's time to re-examine your approach. Instead, develop a diverse repertoire of stories that illustrate different financial principles and solutions.

Unrealistic outcomes presented without proper context can create false expectations. I once observed an adviser telling clients about a portfolio that had achieved exceptional returns during a bull market, without mentioning that such performance was unusual or discussing how the same approach would fare during market downturns. While the story wasn't technically false, it was misleading by omission.

Sarah, a seasoned financial adviser, demonstrates how to avoid manipulation while still telling impactful stories. When discussing investment strategies with a particularly anxious client, she could highlight how another client lost significant assets during a market crash because they weren't working with an adviser. Instead, she shares a more balanced narrative:

"I worked with a client during the 2008 financial crisis who was understandably concerned as markets declined. We revisited their financial plan and discussed both the potential risks of staying invested and the historical evidence for recovery. While I made it clear that I couldn't predict exactly when markets would rebound, we talked through various scenarios. They decided to maintain their long-term strategy while adjusting their emergency fund for greater security. The recovery took time, but by 2011, they were in a stronger position than if they had sold during the downturn. However, I should note that they experienced significant anxiety during that period and staying invested required considerable emotional resilience."

This approach acknowledges both the benefits and challenges of the strategy, respects the client's intelligence, and avoids pressure tactics.

Respecting Client Privacy: The Art of Anonymisation

Stories drawn from real client experiences can be incredibly powerful, but they come with a serious responsibility to protect confidentiality. Client trust is sacred in our profession and breaching it—even unintentionally—can have profound consequences.

I've developed a systematic approach to anonymising client stories that preserves their educational value while protecting privacy:

Change multiple identifying details, not just names. Consider altering age, occupation, family structure, location, and specific financial figures while preserving the core financial principle you're illustrating. This creates what I call "composite characters"—representations that teach accurate financial lessons without exposing any single client's information.

Seek explicit permission when using recognisable success stories, particularly in marketing materials or public presentations. Document this permission and be specific about exactly how and where their story will be shared.

Focus on principles rather than personalities by emphasising the financial concepts at work rather than the individuals involved. This not only protects privacy but often makes the stories more universally applicable.

Here's how this might look in practice:

Original story (problematic): "John and Mary Smith, both professors at the local university, came to me in 2020 with £750,000 in retirement savings. They were concerned about having enough for their daughter's wedding and their own retirement. By reallocating their investments and setting up a specific wedding fund, they were able to pay for the £25,000 wedding last year while their retirement portfolio actually grew to £825,000."

Anonymised version (better): "A professional couple in their 50s approached me with concerns about funding a significant family celebration while staying on track for retirement. They had accumulated substantial retirement savings but weren't sure if they should use those funds for the upcoming expense. We created a separate short-term investment strategy for the celebration while optimising their retirement portfolio for longer-term growth. This approach allowed them to achieve both goals without compromising either, demonstrating the importance of aligning investment timeframes with specific objectives."

The revised version conveys the same financial lesson without revealing identifying details. It's not just about changing names—it's about creating enough distance from the real case that the specific clients couldn't be recognised, while maintaining the authenticity of the financial principle being illustrated.

Ensuring Accuracy in Your Narratives

In our profession, accuracy isn't just a matter of best practice—it's a regulatory and ethical imperative. The Financial Conduct Authority expects advisers to communicate clearly, fairly, and not misleadingly, principles that apply equally to the stories we tell and the data we present.

Accuracy in storytelling requires vigilance and attention to detail:

Verify your facts before sharing any story, particularly when it involves market data, product features, or specific outcomes. When discussing historical market performances, check your figures against reliable sources. If sharing a client success story, review the actual results rather than relying on memory, which can sometimes improve outcomes over time.

Present balanced perspectives by acknowledging both potential benefits and limitations. This doesn't weaken your narrative—it strengthens it by demonstrating thoroughness and honesty. For example, when telling a story about the tax advantages of a particular investment vehicle, also acknowledge its restrictions or situations where it might be less advantageous.

Keep your stories current by regularly reviewing them against changing markets, regulations, and products. A story about inheritance tax planning from five years ago might contain strategies that are no longer optimal under current legislation.

Accuracy extends beyond just getting the numbers right—it's about creating a truthful impression. Consider this example of how the same basic story can be told in ways that create very different impressions:

Less accurate version: "During the COVID market crash, investors who bought into the market made a fortune as stocks rebounded dramatically."

More accurate version: "Following the initial COVID-related market decline in March 2020, many market sectors experienced significant recovery. However, this recovery was uneven across industries, with some technology and healthcare companies seeing substantial gains while travel, hospitality, and certain retail sectors continued to struggle for an extended period. Investors who maintained diversified portfolios or who had the capacity and risk tolerance to selectively invest during this period potentially benefited from the subsequent recovery, though individual results varied considerably based on specific investment choices and timing."

The second version provides a more nuanced and accurate picture of what actually happened, avoiding the oversimplification that could lead to misunderstanding or unrealistic expectations.

Navigating Ethical Dilemmas in Storytelling

Even with the best intentions, financial advisers regularly encounter situations where the ethical path isn't immediately clear. These grey areas require thoughtful navigation rather than rigid rules.

I recall wrestling with such a dilemma early in my advising career. I had a remarkable success story about a client who had achieved financial independence through aggressive early saving and strategic investments. It was a powerful illustration of compound interest and disciplined investing. However, I realised that this client's outcome was exceptionally good due to a combination of fortunate market timing, higher-than-average income, and unusual commitment. While I wanted to inspire other young clients with this story, I worried it might create unrealistic expectations.

After careful consideration, I decided to continue using the story but with important modifications. I explicitly acknowledged the unique factors that contributed to this success and presented it as an aspirational example rather than a typical outcome. I also developed companion stories about more typical client journeys to provide balance.

I tell every investment client, without exception, that their investments **will** fall in value from time to time. Not might or could—they will unless they're in a guaranteed investment vehicle. It is completely unrealistic to expect investments to rise every day. This reality grounds clients and helps manage their expectations. I also reject the old disclaimer that 'investments can fall as well as rise'—for a true long-term investor, temporary declines are not just possible, they are inevitable.

This experience taught me a framework for navigating ethical dilemmas in storytelling that you might find helpful:

Examine your intention with radical honesty. Are you telling this story primarily to help the client make a better decision, or is there an underlying motivation to influence them toward a particular product or service that might benefit you more than them? Your story might be factually accurate but still ethically questionable if your intention isn't aligned with the client's best interest.

Consider both immediate and long-term impact. A story that motivates a client to take action might seem beneficial in the short term, but could it create unrealistic expectations that damage trust later? Conversely, softening realistic risk discussions to avoid frightening a client might seem kind but could leave them unprepared for market volatility.

Be transparent about exceptional circumstances. If your story involves unusual success, significant market timing luck, or rare opportunities, explicitly frame it as such. You might say, "While this outcome was particularly favourable and not typical, the principle of diversification it illustrates applies broadly."

When facing ethical dilemmas, consultation can be invaluable. Discuss challenging cases (without identifying clients) with trusted colleagues or mentors. Sometimes an outside perspective can help clarify the ethical considerations at stake.

Balancing Emotion and Rationality

Storytelling derives much of its power from emotional resonance. Stories that touch our clients' hopes, fears, and values will always be more memorable than dry facts or statistics. Yet this emotional power must be wielded responsibly, particularly in financial advising where decisions have long-term consequences.

The key is not to eliminate emotion from your stories—that would render them ineffective—but rather to ensure that emotion serves understanding rather than obscuring it.

Consider how you might discuss retirement planning with a client who has been postponing saving:

Emotionally manipulative approach: "Let me tell you about a client who thought they had plenty of time to save for retirement. Now they're 70, still working full-time at a physically demanding job because they can't afford to retire, while their friends are enjoying holidays and time with grandchildren. Every day they regret not starting earlier. Is that the future you want?"

Balanced emotional and rational approach: "I'd like to share a story that illustrates why I'm passionate about early retirement planning. I worked with someone who began focused retirement saving in their 50s. They managed to build a meaningful nest egg, but the process required significant lifestyle adjustments that were sometimes challenging. They told me they wished they'd understood earlier how much easier saving would have been if spread over more years.

The mathematics of compound interest clearly shows the advantage of time—even small contributions can grow significantly over decades. But beyond the numbers, what I've observed working with clients near retirement is that those who started earlier typically experience less stress and more choices. Would it be helpful to look at some specific scenarios for your situation, showing how different saving levels might translate to future options?"

The first approach uses fear as a bludgeon, while the second acknowledges the emotional reality of regret while providing context and a path forward. It uses emotion to illuminate the rational argument rather than to overwhelm it.

Some emotional appeals can be particularly powerful in financial storytelling:

Hope and aspiration stories that help clients envision positive futures made possible through sound financial planning can motivate without manipulating.

Relief and security narratives that illustrate how proper planning provided peace of mind during challenging times can be compelling without resorting to fear tactics.

Pride and accomplishment stories that show how disciplined financial decisions led to meaningful achievements can inspire clients to take positive action.

The ethical line is crossed when emotions are triggered primarily to create a sense of urgency or anxiety that leads to hasty decisions, rather than to illustrate important principles that help clients make thoughtful choices.

Building Trust Through Ethical Storytelling

Ethical storytelling isn't just the right thing to do—it's also the foundation of lasting client relationships. In a profession where trust is our most valuable currency, how we tell stories either builds or erodes that essential trust.

I attribute exceptionally high client retention rate to what I call "transparent storytelling." Early in my career, I made the decision never to tell a story that painted an unrealistically rosy picture of investment outcomes. Instead, I developed narratives that acknowledged the complexities of financial markets while emphasising the principles that guide sound decision-making regardless of market conditions.

I've found that clients appreciate honesty above all else. When market downturns inevitably occur, my clients aren't shocked or betrayed—they remember the stories I shared about previous downturns and recoveries. They've been mentally prepared for both the positive and challenging aspects of investing. It's incredibly liberating, eliminates any nasty surprises, and lets me sleep soundly at night.

This approach to storytelling builds what I call "resilient trust"—trust that can withstand market volatility, changing regulations, and even occasional disappointments. It's based on three practices:

Educational storytelling that focuses on empowering clients with knowledge rather than simply steering them toward particular products. This means including stories about potential pitfalls and challenges, not just successes.

Authentic vulnerability in sharing your own experiences, including mistakes you've made or times when your expectations weren't met. This demonstrates humility and humanity, qualities that paradoxically increase rather than diminish client confidence.

Client-centred narratives that are thoughtfully selected based on relevance to the client's specific situation, demonstrating that you see them as individuals rather than applying a one-size-fits-all approach.

Consider crafting a personal statement of storytelling ethics that reflects your values and commitment to clients. Mine includes this promise: "I will never tell a story that I wouldn't be comfortable sharing if the client it concerned were in the room listening."

Ethical Storytelling in a Digital Age

The principles of ethical storytelling remain constant, but digital communication brings unique challenges and opportunities that require special consideration.

In traditional face-to-face advising, stories exist in the moment—shared in a private office, contextualised by the conversation, and responsive to client reactions. In contrast, digital stories can be permanent, public, and consumed without the benefit of your presence to provide nuance or answer questions.

Rebecca, a financial adviser who maintains an active professional social media presence, learned this lesson through experience. "I once shared what I thought was a straightforward client success story on LinkedIn," she explained. "But without the context of our in-person conversations, some readers interpreted it as guaranteeing specific returns. I now approach digital storytelling with much more care, knowing that my stories might reach people with whom I have no established relationship."

Consider these principles for ethical digital storytelling:

Enhanced privacy protection is essential when sharing stories online. Digital content can spread far beyond your intended audience, so use even more stringent anonymisation practices than you would in person. Consider creating entirely fictional composite examples that illustrate financial principles without referencing any specific client.

Clarity about contextual factors helps prevent misinterpretation. When sharing investment success stories online, be explicit about the market conditions, timeframes, and unique circumstances that contributed to the outcome.

Engagement with feedback allows you to clarify and expand on your stories. Monitor comments on your digital content and be prepared to address questions or misunderstandings promptly and transparently.

Consistent values across channels ensure that your digital storytelling reflects the same ethical standards as your in-person communication. It can be tempting to share more dramatic or attention-grabbing stories online to stand out in a crowded digital landscape, but maintaining consistency builds long-term credibility.

If you maintain a blog, social media presence, or newsletter, consider periodically reviewing your digital stories through an ethical lens. Ask yourself: "Does this content still accurately reflect market realities? Have regulations or best practices changed since I shared this story? Is the educational value clear and prominent?"

Practical Example: Ethical Storytelling in Action

Let's examine how these principles might play out in a common advising scenario:

Scenario: A young couple with a baby has come to discuss starting a university fund, but they haven't yet established emergency savings or begun retirement planning.

Unethical Approach: The adviser shares a story about a family whose child couldn't attend their preferred university because they hadn't saved enough, creating anxiety and urgency around opening a fund immediately. The adviser doesn't mention that this story is exceptional or that other financial priorities might be more pressing for this couple.

Ethical Approach: "Before we discuss education funding, I'd like to share a relevant experience. I worked with a family who, like you, had a young child and wanted to give them every advantage. They were committed to funding future education and opened a dedicated account right away. However, six months later, one parent was made redundant. Without adequate emergency savings, they had to use their education fund to cover basic expenses, incurring penalties in the process.

This experience taught me the importance of helping clients establish a comprehensive financial foundation. Research consistently shows that securing your own financial stability first—through emergency savings and retirement planning—ultimately creates more security for your children as well. Would it be helpful if we looked at how we might balance these different priorities in your financial plan?"

This ethical approach:

- Uses a relevant story that acknowledges the clients' priorities
- Presents balanced information about potential pitfalls
- Connects to broader financial principles
- Offers a constructive path forward
- Avoids pressure tactics
- Makes the adviser's reasoning transparent

Summary: Storytelling with Integrity

Ethical storytelling in financial advising isn't about limiting your impact—it's about ensuring that your influence serves your clients' best interests. By committing to truthfulness, transparency, and client-centred relevance, you build the kind of trust that sustains long-term relationships and ultimately leads to better financial outcomes for those you serve.

The stories you share shape not only how clients perceive financial concepts but also how they perceive you as an adviser. When you tell stories with integrity—acknowledging complexities, respecting privacy, balancing emotion with rationality, and adapting thoughtfully to digital contexts—you demonstrate your commitment to ethical practice in every aspect of your work.

I encourage you to regularly reflect on your storytelling practices. Consider keeping a journal of the stories you share frequently, noting how clients respond and whether the stories achieve their intended educational purpose. This kind of reflective practice helps refine your storytelling skills while ensuring they remain aligned with your ethical standards.

Action Step: Review several stories you commonly share with clients, examining them through the ethical frameworks presented in this chapter. For each story, ask yourself:

- Is this story factually accurate and up to date?
- Does it respect client privacy appropriately?
- Does it present a balanced view of both benefits and potential challenges?
- Is it designed primarily to educate and empower rather than to sell or pressure?
- Does it match the specific needs and circumstances of the clients with whom I share it?
- Would I be comfortable having this story scrutinised by colleagues, regulators, or the clients it describes?

By approaching storytelling with this level of ethical awareness, you transform it from merely a communication technique into a manifestation of your professional integrity. In the next chapter, we move from ethical considerations to practical application.

We'll explore specific exercises and techniques to help you develop and refine your storytelling skills, turning these principles into daily practice that enhances your client relationships and elevates your advising effectiveness.

FIVE KEY TAKEAWAYS

1. Ethical storytelling begins with three essential principles: truthfulness (factual accuracy in all narratives), transparency (clarity about your intentions), and relevance (tailoring stories to each client's specific needs).

2. Avoiding manipulative storytelling requires recognising and steering clear of fear-based narratives, product-focused stories that always lead to the same recommendation, and presentations of unrealistic outcomes without proper context.

3. Client privacy must be protected through systematic anonymisation—changing multiple identifying details (not just names), creating composite characters, and focusing on financial principles rather than personalities.

4. Balancing emotion and rationality is crucial. Emotion makes stories memorable but must serve understanding rather than creating undue anxiety or urgency that leads to hasty decisions.

5. Digital storytelling requires heightened ethical awareness as stories become permanent, public, and consumed without your presence to provide context—requiring enhanced privacy protection and explicit clarity about market conditions and circumstances.

CHAPTER 12

Practical Exercises for Financial Advisers

---◇---

"Facts tell, but stories sell"
—Bryan Eisenberg

The only way to get better at storytelling is through practice. Storytelling is both an art and a skill that improves with dedicated practice and thoughtful feedback. In my experience as a financial adviser, I've seen firsthand how developing this ability transforms the way clients perceive and act on financial advice. Even if you don't consider yourself a "natural storyteller," you can develop this skill through consistent practice and the right approach.

In this chapter, I'll share practical exercises, techniques, and frameworks that will help you master the craft of storytelling and weave it seamlessly into your advisory practice. These aren't theoretical concepts—they're hands-on approaches that have worked in real client situations throughout my career.

Developing Your Own Stories: A Step-by-Step Guide

Every impactful story begins with clear purpose. Let me walk you through a process that has helped me craft stories that not only engage clients but also drive home important financial concepts.

Step 1: Identify the Key Message

Begin by clarifying the lesson or insight you want your client to take away. This might seem obvious, but I initially struggled to distil complex financial concepts into a single, memorable message.

Think about the financial principle you're trying to convey. Is it that patience pays off in investing? That diversification protects from unnecessary risk. That starting early makes a significant difference in retirement savings. Choose one core message—trying to communicate too many points in a single story dilutes its impact.

Step 2: Build a Client Persona

Now, consider who would benefit most from your story. Creating a clear mental image of your audience helps you tailor your narrative to their specific concerns and experiences.

For instance, you might envision Sarah, a 35-year-old professional who's concerned about balancing retirement savings with the immediate needs of raising children. By anchoring your story to a specific persona, you'll naturally include details that resonate with similar clients in your practice.

Step 3: Create the Story Framework

A compelling story needs structure—a clear beginning, middle, and end that guides your client through a meaningful journey. Let me show you how this might work with our example of Sarah:

The Challenge begins your story by presenting the problem or situation. "Sarah came to me worried that she couldn't possibly save for retirement while managing her family's day-to-day expenses. With two young children and a mortgage that stretched her budget, retirement saving felt like a luxury she couldn't afford. She was losing sleep wondering if she was failing her family's future."

The Solution shows the steps taken to address the challenge. "Together, we looked at her full financial picture and found small opportunities that, combined, made a meaningful difference. We started with just 3% contributions to her workplace pension to capture her employer's match. Then we created a simple system where any unexpected income—bonuses, tax refunds, birthday gifts—went straight to her retirement fund before she could miss it. Most importantly, we calculated how compounding would work in her favour over the decades ahead."

The Outcome highlights the results, and the lesson learned. "Within three years, Sarah had built a modest but growing retirement fund without significantly changing her lifestyle. What surprised her most wasn't the balance—it was the confidence she felt knowing she was building a foundation for her future while still providing for her family today. She told me, 'For the first time, I don't feel like I'm choosing between today and tomorrow.' Sarah's experience shows that even small, consistent actions can lead to financial confidence when you have a tailored plan."

Notice how this story conveys our key message about starting small and being consistent without explicitly stating it as a dry financial principle. The narrative does the work for us.

Step 4: Test and Refine

Stories improve with use. After sharing your story in client meetings, take a moment to reflect on how it landed. Did the client lean in with interest or seem distracted? Did they ask questions that showed engagement? Did they share a similar experience from their own life?

I use my phone to record or jot down any ideas that come into my head I can expand. I also use it to record observations after using a story: what worked, what didn't, and ideas for refinement. Over time, this practice has helped me develop stories that truly resonate with my clients.

How to Handle Storytelling Resistance

Not every client appreciates a narrative approach. In my experience, I would say about 20% of clients prefer direct, data-driven communications without the "extras" of storytelling. Reading your audience and adapting your approach is just as important as crafting good stories.

You might notice signs that a client isn't engaging with your story—minimal eye contact, fidgeting, or interrupting with direct questions instead of following the narrative. When this happens, don't force the story to its conclusion. Instead, smoothly pivot to a more analytical approach.

I learned this lesson early in my career when I began telling a story about market volatility to a new client but quickly noticed their crossed arms and furrowed brow. Mid-story, I shifted gears: "You know, perhaps it would be more helpful to look at the historical data on this. Let me show you a chart that illustrates exactly what happens during market corrections and the typical recovery patterns."

The client visibly relaxed, and the meeting became much more productive. I used to feel rejected when clients didn't want my stories. Now I see it as valuable information about how they prefer to receive advice.

Consider adopting an "ask first" approach with new clients or those who seem analytical by nature. A simple, "Would you like an example of how this has worked for someone in a similar situation, or would you prefer we focus on the numbers first?" gives clients agency and shows respect for their communication preferences.

Role-Playing Scenarios to Refine Your Techniques

Role-playing may feel uncomfortable at first. I certainly resisted this exercise when I first started developing my storytelling skills. Yet pushing through this discomfort led to significant improvements in my client communications. Role-playing allows you to experiment with different narratives, delivery styles, and pacing in a low-stakes environment before using them with actual clients.

Here's how to make role-playing genuinely useful: Find a colleague who is also committed to improving their storytelling skills. Take turns playing the adviser and the client. When you're the adviser, deliver your story as authentically as you would in a real meeting. When you're the client, provide specific, constructive feedback afterward.

When I was struggling to explain the concept of market volatility to nervous clients, role-playing helped me develop this narrative that has since become one of my most effective tools:

"Imagine you're planning a road trip from London to Edinburgh. Before leaving, you check the weather forecast and see it will be sunny when you depart, rainy in the Midlands, and clearing up as you reach Scotland. Would you cancel your trip because of the rain in the middle? Of course, not—you'd prepare for it and continue your journey.

Investing for retirement is similar. We know there will be sunny periods of growth and rainy periods of decline along the way. Market volatility—those rainy periods—isn't a reason to abandon your journey. It's a natural part of the path to your destination that we prepare for in advance. My job is to help you navigate through those rainy periods without losing sight of your destination.

I've guided many clients through several market downturns over my career. Those who stayed on their journey, even when the rain was heaviest, eventually reached their financial destinations. Those who pulled over and waited for perfect conditions often found themselves significantly delayed or even unable to reach their goals."

This analogy works because it transforms an abstract financial concept into a relatable experience, and it addresses the emotional aspect of investing during volatility without dismissing clients' concerns.

Practical Exercises to Enhance Storytelling Skills

Let me share four exercises that have helped me develop my storytelling abilities, along with guidance on how to incorporate them into your busy practice.

1. Create Multiple Variations of a Story

Financial concepts can be explained in countless ways. The key is finding the approach that resonates with each particular client. Select a common concept like retirement planning and challenge yourself to develop three different stories to explain it—each tailored to a different client profile.

I've created distinct retirement planning narratives for a young professional focused on career growth, a middle-aged parent concerned about university costs, and a near-retiree worried about market volatility. By developing this range, I found myself better equipped to connect with diverse clients.

This doesn't need to be time-consuming. Set aside 30 minutes on a Friday afternoon when client meetings are typically lighter.

Write one variation per week, and within a month, you'll have a versatile set of stories for a key concept.

2. Practice Analogies and Metaphors

Complex financial concepts become accessible when linked to everyday experiences. Spend some time developing analogies for concepts your clients frequently struggle to grasp.

For example, inflation can be described as a balloon slowly losing air, reducing your purchasing power over time. Diversification might be compared to a balanced diet that ensures long-term health by including a variety of nutrients. Compound interest could be likened to planting a tree—modest beginnings that grow exponentially with time.

One of my most effective analogies explains the difference between managing your own investments and working with a professional:

"Many people believe they can manage their own money in retirement, but I have one question: why would they want to? Managing your own finances is like giving yourself a haircut—it may seem simple, but without the right skill and experience, the results can be disastrous.

I've been getting monthly haircuts for over 50 years. That's at least 600 haircuts I've sat through, watching intently in the mirror as the barber cuts my hair. But do you think observing all those haircuts qualifies me to cut my own hair? Of course not.

Investing and financial management require not just knowledge, but the ability to act rationally under pressure, stay objective, and adjust strategies when necessary. Just as a bad self-inflicted haircut can take weeks to fix, a poorly executed financial decision in retirement can have long-term consequences that are difficult to undo."

This analogy works because it's relatable, slightly humorous, and makes a profound point about the difference between observing and doing. Try developing one new analogy each week, testing it with colleagues before using it with clients.

I keep my phone within reach at all times, not just for calls but as my storytelling companion. When inspiration strikes, I immediately capture it—whether it's a fully formed idea or just the seed of a narrative. After client meetings, I take a few minutes to record what resonated and what fell flat in the stories I shared. This digital notebook has become an invaluable resource, helping me refine narratives until they truly connect with clients.

My inspiration comes from the most unexpected sources, particularly entertainment. I'll be relaxing with a film or television show when suddenly a character delivers a line that perfectly encapsulates a financial principle. Without hesitation, I pause the screen, grab my phone, and capture that golden nugget. From there, I craft a financial narrative that brings abstract concepts to life.

Years ago, my wife and I were watching an episode of The Great British Bake Off. A contestant, facing a technical challenge, remarked: "It's not about following the recipe perfectly—it's about understanding why each ingredient matters". That single line provided me with another way to explain investment diversification. I developed it into an analogy comparing portfolio construction to baking, explaining how each asset class serves a specific purpose—some for stability (flour), others for growth (leavening), and some for protection (salt). Clients who previously glazed over during technical discussions now nod with understanding.

This approach might seem peculiar, but I've learned to trust these moments of clarity whenever they appear. The key is to capture every flash of inspiration immediately, whether it arrives during a documentary, a conversation with friends, or even while reading fiction. These everyday connections transform complex financial concepts into accessible stories that clients not only understand but remember and act upon. What might initially seem like an unusual parallel to you could become the perfect bridge to understanding for your client. It is worth cultivating a heightened awareness for these flashes of inspiration, training yourself to recognise and capture them before they fade.

3. Record and Review Your Stories

This exercise requires vulnerability but yields tremendous insights. Use your phone to record yourself delivering a story, then listen with a critical ear. Pay attention to your pacing—are you rushing through important points? Notice your tone—does it convey confidence and empathy? Consider your language—are you using jargon that might confuse clients?

When I first tried this exercise, I became aware of my speech patterns and noticed certain filler phrases appearing frequently throughout my delivery. This mindfulness about language choices allowed me to communicate more clearly and professionally, focusing on precision rather than repetitive expressions.

If recording yourself feels too uncomfortable, start by practicing in front of a mirror, focusing on your facial expressions and gestures. These non-verbal elements significantly impact how your story is received. It might feel unusual at first but refining your communication skills yields tremendous results. At its core, financial advising is about effective communication—the more clearly and memorably you convey complex concepts, the more likely clients are to trust your guidance and commit to a long-term professional relationship.

4. Experiment with Visual Aids

Stories become even more powerful when paired with thoughtful visual elements, as shown in the examples of the crystal ball, the two beakers, and the noise-cancelling headphones. When explaining compound interest, try drawing a simple curve that starts flat and then steepens dramatically. As you tell a story about patient investing, trace your finger along the curve, showing how the early years yield modest growth while later years bring exponential results.

I've created what I call "story cards"—simple visual aids that complement my most frequently used narratives. For my story about market volatility, I have a card showing the historical pattern of market recoveries following major downturns. As I share my road trip analogy, I slide the card across the table, creating a powerful moment of visual affirmation.

You don't need elaborate presentations—sometimes a simple drawing on paper can be more engaging than a polished slide. The key is ensuring the visual element enhances rather than distracts from your narrative.

Feedback Mechanisms for Continuous Improvement

Storytelling skills develop through a cycle of practice, feedback, refinement, and more practice. Let's explore how to create effective feedback loops that propel your storytelling forward.

Client feedback provides the most valuable insights, but gathering it requires subtlety. Rather than asking directly about your storytelling, which might feel awkward, ask broader questions about clarity and understanding. After sharing a story, you might ask, "Did that example help clarify the concept?" or "What aspects of our discussion today did you find most helpful?"

Watch for non-verbal feedback as well. When clients lean forward, nod, or maintain eye contact during your story, they're engaged. When they reference your story later in the conversation or in subsequent meetings, you know it resonated deeply.

Peer feedback offers another valuable perspective. Consider forming a small group with other advisers who are committed to improving their communication skills. Meet monthly to share stories and provide constructive feedback to one another. In these sessions, focus on specific elements: Was the message clear? Did the story flow logically? Were there emotional touchpoints that resonated?

Self-reflection completes the feedback loop. After client meetings, take a few moments to consider: Did my story achieve its purpose? Which parts seemed to connect most strongly? What might I adjust for next time? This habit of reflection helps you internalise lessons from each client interaction.

I keep a "storytelling journal" where I document which stories worked well with different client types. Over time, patterns emerged that helped me match stories more effectively to client personalities and concerns. I found that analytical clients responded best to stories with specific numbers and clear cause-and-effect relationships, while more emotionally driven clients connected with narratives that emphasised feelings of security and accomplishment.

Continuous Practice: Turning Stories into Tools

To truly embed storytelling into your practice, it needs to become second nature—a tool you reach for instinctively rather than something that requires conscious effort each time.

Developing a story library accelerates this process. Create a simple system—whether digital or physical—to organise your stories by financial concept, client type, and purpose. Include notes about which stories have worked well in specific situations and any refinements you've made over time.

When preparing for client meetings, I quickly mentally review relevant stories, refreshing them in my mind before the conversation. It's like having a mental toolbox at my disposal, allowing me to select precisely the right story or analogy that will resonate with each client's unique situation and communication style.

Don't let your stories become stale. Financial markets evolve, regulations change, and cultural references lose relevance. Schedule quarterly reviews of your most frequently used stories to ensure they remain accurate and resonant. This doesn't need to be time-consuming—a quick 30-minute audit can keep your storytelling fresh and effective.

Finally, stay curious about how others use storytelling. When you attend industry events or professional development sessions, pay attention to speakers who engage you with their narratives. What techniques do they employ? How do they structure their stories? How do they use pace, pause, and emphasis to create impact? Borrow what works and adapt it to your own style.

Practice Makes Progress

Storytelling isn't perfected overnight—it's a skill that develops through consistent practice and reflection. Each time you craft a narrative, role-play a scenario, or refine your delivery, you're building capacity that enhances your client relationships and distinguishes your practice. Remember that the goal isn't perfection but progress. Even the most seasoned storytellers continue to refine their craft. What matters is that you begin the journey and commit to ongoing improvement.

Start today. Choose a financial concept that you frequently discuss with clients, craft a story around it using the framework we've explored and use it in your next client meeting. Notice what works, refine your approach, and try again. Each iteration brings you closer to mastering the art of storytelling.

In my years as a financial adviser, I've seen how developing strong storytelling skills fundamentally changes how clients understand and act on advice. The transformation doesn't just enhance communication—it creates deeper client relationships built on understanding and trust.

Storytelling is a skill that improves with practice, but practice alone isn't enough—you need to measure what's working and refine your approach. A well-crafted story may feel engaging, but how do you know if it's truly resonating with clients? Are they understanding complex concepts more easily? Are they making better financial decisions as a result?

In the next chapter, we move from practising storytelling to measuring its impact. By tracking engagement, gathering feedback, and assessing the effectiveness of different storytelling techniques, you can ensure that your narratives aren't just compelling but also meaningful and results driven. Understanding what works—and what doesn't—allows you to continuously improve, making every client interaction more impactful.

FIVE KEY TAKEAWAYS

1. Every effective story follows a clear framework: identify the key message, build a client persona, create a structured narrative with beginning (challenge), middle (solution), and end (outcome), then test and refine based on client reactions.

2. Reading your audience is crucial—not all clients appreciate storytelling, and it's important to recognise when to pivot to a more analytical approach rather than forcing a narrative that isn't resonating.

3. Creating your personal "story library" with multiple variations for different client types allows you to select precisely the right analogy for each situation, making your communication more targeted and effective.

4. Unexpected sources of inspiration—particularly entertainment, films, and everyday experiences—can provide powerful analogies that transform complex financial concepts into accessible stories clients remember and act upon.

5. Continuous improvement requires creating feedback loops through client responses, peer feedback, and self-reflection, helping you match stories more effectively to client personalities and refine your delivery over time.

CHAPTER 13

Observing the Impact of Storytelling

"The art of conversation is the art of hearing as well as being heard."
—William Hazlitt

You can't improve what you don't observe. In the previous chapter, we explored practical exercises for developing your storytelling skills. Now we turn our attention to a critical but often overlooked aspect: being mindful of how your stories affect client understanding, engagement, and decision-making. While crafting compelling narratives is essential, paying attention to their effectiveness allows you to thoughtfully refine your approach and appreciate the tangible value storytelling brings to your practice.

Beyond Intuition: The Case for Mindful Observation

Many advisers rely solely on intuition to gauge whether their stories are effective. While your instincts certainly play a role, being intentionally observant provides insights that gut feelings alone cannot deliver.

Early in my career, I assumed that if clients nodded and smiled during meetings, my communication was effective. It wasn't until I began paying closer attention to what happened after our meetings that I discovered the gap between apparent understanding and actual implementation of advice. Some clients who seemed engaged during meetings never took action, while others who asked challenging questions often became my most committed clients.

This revelation led me to develop a more thoughtful approach to observing how my stories landed with clients. The insights gained have transformed not just my storytelling approach but the fundamental client relationships in my practice.

Signs That Matter: What to Look For

Rather than measuring storytelling in isolation, I pay attention to its impact across the entire client journey. This comprehensive approach reveals how storytelling influences client behaviour while improving outcomes.

Understanding Indicators

These observations help assess whether clients genuinely grasp financial concepts after hearing your stories:

- **Concept Recall** – Can clients accurately explain key financial principles weeks after you've shared a story? I occasionally ask clients to summarise previous discussions, noting which story-delivered concepts they retain versus those explained through traditional methods.
- **Question Quality** – The thoughtfulness and relevance of client questions serve as indicators of understanding. Notice whether questions become more insightful over

time, suggesting deeper comprehension of financial concepts.

- **Application to Personal Situations** – When clients independently apply concepts from your stories to their own circumstances ("This is like the gardening analogy you shared, but in my situation..."), they demonstrate true understanding.

I've found that clients who receive concepts through stories tend to have notably better recall compared to my previous technical explanation approach. Their questions evolve from basic clarifications to thoughtful explorations of how concepts apply to their unique circumstances.

Decision-Making Indicators

These observations help assess how storytelling influences client decision-making:

- **Implementation Patterns** – Do clients tend to follow through on recommendations after hearing relevant stories? I've noticed that recommendations supported by relevant stories see significantly higher implementation rates than those explained through data alone.

- **Decision Timeframes** – How quickly do clients make decisions after hearing stories versus receiving traditional explanations? I've observed that storytelling typically reduces the time clients need to make decisions, particularly for complex financial choices like retirement planning or estate strategies.

- **Expressed Confidence** – Listen for how clients describe their confidence in decisions. Those made after story-based explanations often come with expressions like "I feel comfortable with this approach" or "This makes sense to me now."

- **Behaviour During Volatility** – Perhaps most importantly, observe how consistent clients remain with their financial plans during market turbulence. I've noticed that clients who received story-based explanations of market cycles are much less likely to panic and request portfolio changes during downturns.

Relationship Indicators

These observations help assess how storytelling influences long-term client relationships:

- **Meeting Engagement** – Notice the quality of client participation during meetings. Does storytelling increase active discussion versus passive listening? I've found that meetings where I use relevant stories tend to involve much more client participation.

- **Time Awareness** – How often do clients lose track of time during your meetings? When meetings where storytelling is a primary communication method run over scheduled time, it's usually because clients are genuinely engaged—a positive indicator.

- **Referral Language** – When clients refer others, do they specifically mention your communication style? Listen for comments like "She explains things in a way that really makes sense" or references to specific stories you've shared.

- **Client Longevity** – Over time, notice whether clients who receive story-based explanations tend to remain with your practice longer than those who don't. I've observed a meaningful decrease in client turnover since implementing thoughtful storytelling approaches.

Creating an Observation Approach That Works

Being mindful of storytelling impact doesn't require complex systems or burdensome processes. Here's how I've implemented a straightforward approach that delivers valuable insights without overwhelming administrative work:

The Post-Meeting Reflection

After significant client meetings, I take a few moments to reflect on our conversation. I consider things like:

- Did the client seem to understand the key concepts?
- What was the quality and relevance of their questions?
- How engaged were they throughout our discussion?
- How confident did they seem in any decisions made?
- Which stories generated the most engagement?

This takes just a couple of minutes after each meeting, but the accumulated insights have been invaluable for refining my storytelling approach.

Digital Engagement Observations

For advisers who communicate through digital channels, additional indicators become available:

- Do story-based emails receive more responses than technical ones?
- Which types of content on your website keep visitors reading longer?
- Do narrative social media posts generate more engagement than purely factual ones?
- Are story-based video explanations watched to completion more often?

I consistently find that narrative-driven communications receive substantially higher engagement across all digital channels compared to primarily technical content.

Implementation Awareness

To better understand the connection between storytelling and client action, I've become more intentional about noting:

- Which explanation approaches tend to lead to client action?
- How long clients typically take to move from explanation to decision
- Whether recommendations are fully implemented, partially implemented, or not implemented
- Common reasons clients give when they don't implement recommendations

This awareness has revealed that complex recommendations explained through stories are much more likely to be implemented than those explained through traditional approaches alone.

Appreciating the Financial Impact of Storytelling

While improved client understanding and engagement are valuable outcomes in themselves, the business impact of effective storytelling is also worth noting. By paying attention to patterns in your practice, you may notice several beneficial developments:

New Client Relationships

After implementing thoughtful storytelling approaches, many advisers notice an improvement in their ability to connect with prospective clients. This often leads to more new client relationships forming from initial consultations.

With the significant lifetime value of each client relationship, even a modest improvement in connection with prospects can have a substantial positive impact on your practice.

Client Retention

Client retention directly affects practice stability and profitability. By observing retention patterns, you may notice that clients who receive story-based explanations tend to remain with your practice longer.

This extended relationship duration represents additional years of service and revenue, significantly enhancing the lifetime value of each client relationship.

Deeper Client Relationships

Clients who thoroughly understand financial concepts through well-crafted stories often prove more willing to consolidate their financial matters with a trusted adviser. You might notice an increase in the proportion of clients' total financial lives that they entrust to your care.

This deepening of relationships typically leads to a more comprehensive service offering and greater overall client satisfaction.

The Profound Impact of Natural Referrals

Referrals represent the most genuine form of client appreciation and perhaps the most meaningful indicator that your storytelling approach is truly connecting. When clients spontaneously recommend you to friends, family, or colleagues, they're validating both your expertise and your ability to communicate complex concepts in an accessible way.

I've found that listening carefully to how clients describe you when making referrals offers profound insights into the value of your storytelling approach. The language they use tells you exactly what they value most about your service.

The Validation of Communication-Based Referrals

In my experience, the most powerful compliment clients ever give me is when they say, "You explain things in a way that's easy to understand" or "You never use confusing jargon." These statements validate not just what I do, but how I do it. They confirm that storytelling isn't merely a communication technique—it's a fundamental component of the value I provide.

When a client tells a friend, "My adviser explains financial concepts using everyday examples that actually make sense," they're highlighting something remarkable—that clarity of communication is distinctive enough to be a defining characteristic worth sharing. In a profession where technical expertise is expected, the ability to translate that expertise into understanding becomes a significant differentiator.

I recall a client who invited his brother to join our annual review meeting. At the end, the brother shook my hand and said, "I've been working with another adviser for years, and I still don't understand half of what he tells me. In just one hour, you've made several concepts clear that he never could." Within a week, he had transferred his portfolio to my practice. The catalyst wasn't superior technical knowledge—it was the ability to make that knowledge accessible through storytelling.

The Language of Referrals

Pay particular attention to the specific language clients use when referring others:

- **"She makes complicated things simple"** – This suggests your stories are successfully translating complex concepts into understandable terms.

- **"He uses examples that relate to real life"** – This indicates your analogies and metaphors are connecting financial concepts to everyday experiences.
- **"For the first time, I actually understand how my investments work"** – This powerful statement reflects the transformative impact of effective storytelling on client comprehension.
- **"She never talks down to you"** – This suggests your stories create a sense of partnership rather than hierarchy, respecting the client's intelligence while making concepts accessible.

When you hear these types of comments, you're receiving confirmation that your storytelling approach isn't just appreciated—it's remarkable enough to motivate clients to share their experience with others.

Referral Quality and Conversion

I've noticed that referrals based on communication quality tend to arrive with a different energy than other types of referrals. The prospective clients often come already predisposed to engage with you because they've been told specifically about your communication style. Their first question isn't typically about performance or fees, but rather, "My friend says you're great at explaining investments. I've never really understood how my portfolio works—can you help me?"

These communication-based referrals typically convert into client relationships more naturally and with greater commitment. The prospects arrive with the expectation that you'll help them understand their financial situation, often after experiences with advisers who left them confused or overwhelmed. Their desire for clarity creates an immediate opportunity for your storytelling approach to demonstrate value.

Cultivating Communication-Based Referrals

While referrals should always develop organically, you can gently nurture communication-based referrals by:

- **Reinforcing clarity as a core value** – When clients express appreciation for your explanations, acknowledge that making complex concepts understandable is a central part of your approach.
- **Providing shareable insights** – Create simple explanations of common financial concepts that clients can share with friends who might be struggling with the same issues.
- **Asking revealing questions** – When meeting with a referred prospect, questions like "What did [the referring client] tell you about how we work together?" often reveals valuable insights about which aspects of your communication style resonated enough to be shared.
- **Expressing genuine appreciation** – When clients refer others based on your communication style, acknowledge how meaningful this specific type of endorsement is to you.

The Chain Reaction of Communication Excellence

The impact of communication-based referrals extends beyond individual new client relationships. Each time a client describes you as someone who "explains things clearly," they're reinforcing the value of effective communication in financial advising—not just for your practice, but for the profession as a whole.

I've found that advisers who become known for their storytelling and clear communication often develop a distinctive reputation in their communities. Prospects begin to arrive having heard specifically about this aspect of the adviser's approach, creating a virtuous cycle where communication excellence becomes a central element of the practice's identity and value proposition.

The Emotional Power Behind the Words

Clients rarely remember every word you say — but they remember how those words made them feel. That's why *how* you say something is just as important as *what* you say. When your explanations create clarity, when your stories calm panic or spark confidence, you're not just informing — you're transforming.

As Maya Angelou famously put it:

"People will forget what you said, people will forget what you did, but people will never forget how you made them feel."

In financial advice, the right words don't just transfer knowledge — they change experience. That's the real power of storytelling.

The Power of Becoming The Adviser They Talk About

Clients don't just want expertise — they want to *feel* something from the way you explain things. When they walk away from a meeting thinking, *"Why hasn't anyone ever explained it like that before?"*, you've done more than educate them — you've elevated the experience.

That feeling turns clients into raving fans. They tell their friends not because you dazzled them with charts, but because you made the complex feel simple and human. Clients never forget how you made them feel — especially when you replaced fear with clarity, or confusion with confidence. That's the story they carry into conversations: *"You have to talk to my adviser — they just explain it so easily."*

And that's how your story starts spreading without you ever needing to ask.

The greatest validation of your storytelling approach isn't found in client satisfaction surveys or retention statistics—it's in those powerful moments when clients voluntarily share with someone they care about: "You should talk to my adviser. For the first time in my life, I actually understand what's happening with my money." There is perhaps no greater confirmation that your storytelling has truly made a difference.

Overall Practice Vitality

The combined effect of these improvements can be transformative for an advisory practice. Without implementing complex measurement systems, simply being mindful of these patterns can help you appreciate how storytelling contributes to:

- Building more new client relationships
- Extending the duration of existing relationships
- Deepening the scope of services provided
- Generating more natural referrals

These benefits come not from fundamentally changing your advisory approach, but simply from communicating your expertise more effectively through thoughtful storytelling.

From Observation to Refinement: Creating a Continuous Improvement Approach

Being observant only creates value when you use those insights to improve your storytelling approach. Here's how I've implemented a continuous refinement cycle based on what I've noticed:

Periodic Story Review

Every few months, I reflect on which stories seem to have the greatest impact:

- Which stories consistently help clients understand complex concepts?
- Which stories don't seem to resonate as well as I'd expected?
- Which financial concepts still seem challenging for clients to grasp?
- Do different types of clients respond differently to various storytelling approaches?

For stories that don't seem to connect well, I consider:

- Is the core analogy relevant to this type of client?
- Does the story structure clearly communicate the key concept?
- Does the story connect emotionally with what matters to clients?
- Does the story naturally suggest next steps for implementation?

This reflection often reveals simple adjustments that can transform an underperforming story into an effective communication tool.

Exploring Alternative Approaches

For key financial concepts, I sometimes develop different story approaches and notice which ones seem most effective. By paying attention to how clients respond, I continuously improve my storytelling repertoire.

For example, when explaining investment risk, I experimented with different analogies—one involving weather patterns, another about mountain climbing, and a third using a journey metaphor. Over time, I noticed that the journey story resulted in better client understanding and more appropriate risk decisions, though the mountain climbing analogy often created a stronger emotional impact.

Noticing Patterns Across Client Types

Being observant allows you to notice which stories resonate with specific types of clients. I've become more attuned to how story effectiveness might vary across:

- Client age and life stage
- Professional background and education
- Apparent risk tolerance and financial knowledge
- Communication preferences

This awareness reveals patterns that help tailor storytelling approaches. For instance, I've noticed that clients from technical backgrounds often respond better to stories with clear logical relationships and specific examples, while clients from teaching or caring professions often connect more strongly with stories involving personal growth and future generations.

Fostering a Culture of Thoughtful Storytelling in Your Practice

For advisers in larger practices, encouraging collective observation of storytelling effectiveness multiplies the benefits while providing comparative insights to accelerate improvement.

Team Storytelling Awareness

Consider implementing these practice-wide approaches:

- Regular sharing of stories that seem particularly effective with clients
- Informal peer feedback on storytelling approaches

- Occasional team discussions about which explanation methods seem most effective
- Collaborative development of stories for new financial concepts or changing market conditions

By comparing observations across different advisers explaining the same concepts, patterns emerge that help identify the most effective storytelling approaches for your specific client base.

In my experience, advisers often face two consistent challenges: getting in front of new people and knowing what to say when they do. The first meeting is where most of the conversion power lies — and too often, it's where advisers rely on technical fluency instead of emotional clarity. The contents of this book are designed to give you the best possible chance of having a first meeting that not only informs but *connects* — where the prospective client walks away thinking, *"That made more sense than anything I've heard before."*

By embedding these storytelling principles into team culture, you equip everyone in the practice with the ability to turn everyday conversations into trust-building, relationship-starting moments.

Development Focused on Client Response

Rather than generic storytelling training, focus development efforts on addressing specific areas where clients seem to struggle with understanding. For instance, if several advisers notice clients have difficulty grasping investment risk concepts, develop and share better stories for explaining risk.

This targeted approach transforms professional development from an abstract exercise to a practical response to observed client needs.

The Future of Client-Centred Storytelling

As financial services becomes increasingly digitised, new opportunities emerge for understanding storytelling impact:

- More personalised communications based on observed client preferences
- Digital platforms that allow more consistent delivery of key stories
- Enhanced client feedback channels to better understand what resonates
- Greater ability to tailor stories to specific client circumstances

While technology creates new possibilities, the fundamental principle remains unchanged: paying attention to how clients respond to your stories allows you to continuously improve your communication effectiveness.

Putting Observation into Action

Begin your journey toward more mindful storytelling with these steps:

1. **Notice Key Indicators** – Become more aware of how clients respond to different explanation approaches.
2. **Create Simple Reflection Habits** – Develop straightforward ways to capture your observations without creating administrative burden.
3. **Establish Mental Baselines** – Form a general sense of your current effectiveness to provide comparison points.
4. **Schedule Periodic Reviews** – Set aside time occasionally to reflect on what you've observed.
5. **Apply Insights** – Use your observations to refine your storytelling approach.

The journey to storytelling mastery combines the art of narrative with the wisdom of observation. By thoughtfully noting the impact of your stories, you transform them from occasional communication tools into strategic assets that enhance client relationships and practice vitality.

In the final chapter, we'll explore how to integrate everything you've learned about storytelling into a cohesive approach that defines your practice, differentiates your client experience, and cements your legacy as a trusted adviser who truly connects with clients.

FIVE KEY TAKEAWAYS

1. Mindful observation of how your stories land with clients provides deeper insights than intuition alone, revealing the gap between apparent understanding during meetings and actual implementation afterwards.

2. Three types of indicators help assess storytelling impact: understanding indicators (concept recall, question quality, application to personal situations), decision-making indicators (implementation patterns, decision timeframes, behaviour during volatility), and relationship indicators (meeting engagement, referral language).

3. The post-meeting reflection process—taking just a few minutes to consider client understanding, engagement and confidence—creates valuable insights for refining your storytelling approach without requiring complex systems.

4. Communication-based referrals are particularly powerful validation of your storytelling effectiveness—when clients specifically mention your ability to explain complex concepts clearly, it confirms that your approach creates distinctive value.

5. Creating a continuous improvement cycle through periodic story reviews, exploring alternative approaches, and noticing which stories resonate with different client types helps transform storytelling from an occasional technique to a strategic practice asset.

CHAPTER 14

Conclusion

"Facts don't persuade, feelings do. And stories are the best way to get at those feelings."
—*Tom Asacker*

Every great financial plan begins with a story—yours, your client's, and the journey you take together.

As we reach the final pages of our exploration together, it's worth reflecting on the journey we've taken through the landscape of storytelling for financial advisers. Like all meaningful journeys, ours has had a clear purpose: to transform how you communicate with clients, helping them grasp complex concepts and inspiring them to take action toward their financial goals. The techniques we've explored aren't merely communication skills—they're bridges of understanding between your expertise and your clients' needs.

The Story of Your Development

Throughout this book, we've explored how storytelling transforms abstract financial concepts into relatable, memorable narratives that inspire trust, clarity, and confidence.

You've discovered techniques for crafting compelling stories, creating relatable characters, simplifying complex ideas through analogies, and delivering narratives that resonate on both intellectual and emotional levels.

Think back to where you were when you first opened these pages. Perhaps you already sensed the power of stories but lacked a framework for using them effectively. Or maybe you were sceptical about whether storytelling could truly enhance your practice. Wherever you began, you've now acquired tools that can fundamentally change how clients experience your guidance.

This progression—from curiosity to knowledge to implementation—represents a story in itself. It's a narrative of professional growth that parallels the financial journeys your clients undertake with your guidance. Just as they might feel uncertain before gaining clarity through your stories, you may have questioned whether these techniques would truly make a difference in your practice. Now, equipped with concrete methods and approaches, you stand ready to transform client relationships through the power of narrative.

Why Storytelling Transcends Technical Expertise

Professional qualifications and technical knowledge form the foundation of your career as a financial adviser. The hours spent studying for exams, analysing market data, and understanding complex financial instruments are essential. Yet even the most technically proficient adviser may struggle to create meaningful impact without the ability to communicate that expertise effectively to clients.

Consider how often clients make decisions based not on what they know, but on what they feel. Research consistently shows that financial choices—from investment strategies to retirement planning—are driven predominantly by emotion rather than logic. Despite our best efforts to present compelling data and rational arguments, human beings are emotional creatures first and foremost. When faced with financial decisions, clients' fears, hopes, dreams, and anxieties typically overpower even the most carefully constructed logical arguments. This emotional primacy in decision-making isn't a flaw to be corrected, but rather a fundamental aspect of human nature that we must acknowledge and work with. This is precisely why storytelling matters so profoundly in our profession.

Stories serve as the bridge between the rational and emotional aspects of financial decision-making. While your charts demonstrate historical market recoveries, it's the story of a client who remained invested through market turbulence that gives frightened investors the courage to stay the course. Your explanation of inheritance tax planning might be technically flawless, but it's the narrative about a family legacy preserved through careful planning that motivates clients to take action.

This ability to translate technical concepts into relatable stories isn't a supplementary skill—it is fundamental to success in financial advising. While data points inform, narratives transform. The most successful advisers master both the technical and narrative aspects of their profession, recognising that each strengthens the other.

The Ripple Effect of Your Stories

The true power of storytelling extends far beyond individual client meetings. When you share a story that resonates, you create ripples that extend into your clients' futures and, potentially, across generations.

That analogy about pound-cost averaging might be the mental framework your client relies on during market volatility twenty years from now. The story you tell about retirement planning could become the lesson your client passes to their children, creating a legacy of financial wisdom. The metaphor you use to explain risk might give a client the language to make confident decisions long after they've forgotten the specific numbers and calculations you presented.

This ripple effect means your influence as a storytelling adviser extends beyond the immediate financial plan. You become part of your clients' internal dialogue about money—the voice of reason and perspective they hear when facing financial decisions or challenges. This profound level of influence comes with responsibility, which is why we've emphasised the ethical foundations of storytelling throughout our journey together.

Creating Your Storytelling Legacy

As a financial adviser, you occupy a unique position in your clients' lives. You're not just managing money—you're helping write the stories of their futures. Every recommendation you make, every strategy you suggest, represents a potential chapter in their journey. By wrapping these recommendations in compelling narratives, you transform abstract concepts into meaningful action steps that clients can embrace and own.

Consider Claire, an adviser who began her career focused almost exclusively on technical expertise. She relied on charts and figures to communicate with clients, priding herself on the accuracy of her projections and the depth of her market knowledge. Yet despite her undeniable expertise, she noticed that clients often left meetings confused or hesitant to implement her recommendations.

The turning point came during a particularly challenging market period. Rather than overwhelming anxious clients with more data, Claire decided to share a simple story about a couple who had navigated similar volatility by staying invested. She described their initial fears, their consideration of moving to cash, and ultimately, how their patience was rewarded as markets recovered. To her surprise, this story sparked immediate recognition in her clients. They understood the emotional cycle of investing in a way that no chart had ever conveyed.

From that day forward, Claire began intentionally weaving stories into her practice. She collected examples from her own experience and created analogies that made complex ideas accessible. She became known not just for her financial acumen but for her ability to make difficult concepts relatable. Her client retention improved, referrals increased, and most importantly, her clients began implementing her advice with greater confidence and consistency.

Claire's transformation illustrates what's possible when an adviser embraces storytelling as a core professional skill. Her journey could be yours—a progression from technical expert to trusted guide whose stories illuminate the path to financial wellbeing.

Continuing Your Storytelling Journey

Becoming a master storyteller is not a destination but a continuous journey. Markets change, client concerns evolve, and your own experiences grow richer with time. Each of these elements provides fresh material to refine and expand your storytelling repertoire.

To continue developing as a storytelling adviser:

Remain endlessly curious about the world beyond finance. Great stories often emerge from unexpected sources—literature, history, science, or everyday observations. Notice how skilled communicators in other fields create connections and convey complex ideas through narrative. A documentary about mountain climbing might inspire a perfect analogy for long-term investing. A gardening experience could yield insights about patience and growth that illuminate retirement planning.

Build and nurture your personal story library. Create a system—whether digital or physical—for capturing and organising the narratives that resonate most powerfully with clients. Review and refine these stories regularly, noting which elements connect most deeply with different types of clients. Consider categorising your stories by both financial concept (retirement planning, investment risk, inheritance planning) and emotional need (confidence, security, legacy, freedom).

Collaborate with colleagues to expand your narrative approach. Share stories with trusted peers and invite their feedback. Listen to how they explain complex concepts and borrow elements that might enhance your own technique. Consider forming a storytelling circle with other advisers who are committed to developing this skill, meeting regularly to practice new narratives and refine existing ones.

Adapt your storytelling to emerging communication channels. While face-to-face conversations remain invaluable, today's clients engage through multiple media. Experiment with how your stories translate to written communications, social media, podcasts, webinars, or short videos. Each medium presents unique opportunities and constraints for storytelling, requiring thoughtful adaptation while maintaining the core narrative power.

Teach and mentor others in narrative skills. Nothing solidifies your own mastery like helping others develop. By guiding colleagues in storytelling techniques, you'll refine your understanding while contributing to the elevation of our profession as a whole. The questions and insights that emerge from teaching often lead to deeper awareness of your own storytelling practice.

From Understanding to Action

The stories you share with clients create bridges between understanding and action. They provide the crucial link between knowing what should be done and actually doing it. This transformative power deserves cultivation and care.

As you reflect on the techniques and approaches, we've explored together, consider how you'll integrate them into your practice. Rather than attempting to implement everything at once, focus on progressive mastery:

Begin by identifying one financial concept that your clients consistently struggle to grasp. Craft a single story or analogy that illuminates this concept and use it deliberately in your next client conversations. Notice the responses—the questions that follow, the moments of recognition, the decisions that emerge. Refine your narrative based on these observations.

Next, expand your focus to include the emotional dimension of financial decisions. Develop stories that address not just understanding but also the feelings of uncertainty, hope, or concern that influence client choices. Practice delivering these narratives with appropriate pacing and tone, creating space for clients to connect intellectually and emotionally.

Gradually build a repertoire of stories for different concepts and client situations, always focusing on quality rather than quantity. A handful of well-crafted, versatile narratives will serve you better than dozens of underdeveloped examples.

Finally, create a system for capturing new story ideas and client responses. The most powerful additions to your storytelling toolkit will often emerge unexpectedly—from client interactions, personal experiences, or observations. By maintaining awareness of these opportunities, you'll continuously enrich your narrative approach.

Your Invitation to Begin

As our journey through these pages concludes, yours as a storytelling adviser truly begins. The techniques and approaches we've explored together await your unique application. The examples and frameworks provided throughout this book are merely starting points—your personal experiences, client relationships, and professional wisdom will transform them into something distinctively yours.

In the years to come, your clients may not remember every detail of their financial plan, but they will remember the stories that gave them courage to stay invested, the analogies that helped them understand complex concepts, and the narratives that made their financial journey meaningful. That is your legacy as a storytelling financial adviser.

I invite you to begin today with a simple step. Review your calendar for the coming week and identify one client meeting where a story might enhance understanding or inspire action. Prepare a narrative specifically for this client and situation, drawing on the techniques we've explored. After the meeting, reflect on what worked well and what you might adjust next time. This single step begins a practice that can transform your client relationships and elevate your professional impact.

Remember that becoming a masterful storyteller is itself a story—one of growth, learning, and transformation. Like any worthwhile journey, it begins with a single step and unfolds over time, revealing new insights and opportunities along the way. The technical expertise you've worked so hard to develop deserves to be shared in a way that moves and motivates your clients. Let storytelling be the bridge that connects your knowledge to their needs, your expertise to their understanding, and your guidance to their goals.

Now, turn the page and begin writing your own story of transformation through the power of storytelling. Your clients—and your practice—await.

INDEX

A

Abstract concepts, 15, 53, 64, 69, 75, 79, 161, 162, 200, 207, 234, 262
Accuracy, 214, 215, 226, 262
Achievements, 29, 118, 219
Active listening, 54
Adaptation, 48, 188, 264
Advisory practice, 14, 15, 227, 252
Analogies, 40, 42, 46, 50, 243, 260, 261, 263, 264, 265, 266
  building trust, 180
  crafting compelling narratives, 53, 54, 55, 56, 58, 60, 61, 62, 64
  impact of storytelling, 249, 253, 254
  practical exercises, 232, 233, 234, 236, 238, 240
  psychological dimensions of of financial erosion, 124
  setting the scene, 80
  simplifying complex concepts, 129, 131, 132, 135, 139, 143, 145, 150, 161, 162, 163, 171
  storytelling across different media, 200
  Young professionals, 129
Analytical thinkers, 28, 30, 37
Anchoring, 103
Anonymisation, 68, 213
Anonymity, 68
Anxiety, 4, 16, 135, 144, 178, 184, 212, 219, 222, 226
  building trust, 174, 175
  common client concerns, 70
  market volatility, 117, 136
  power of stories, 42, 47
  retirement planning, 176
  setting the scene, 81, 88, 119
Artificial Intelligence, 47, 198, 201
Asacker, Tom, 259
Aspirations, 13, 38, 52, 53, 54, 71, 72, 76, 79, 81, 109, 116, 122, 124, 167, 173, 188, 189
Asset allocation, 55, 134, 162
Assets, 3, 33, 34, 35, 66, 121, 136, 142, 160, 162, 212, 234, 257, 258
Authenticity, 165, 166
Awareness, 244, 246, 254

B

Background information, 30
Balanced portfolio, 11, 69, 158
Banking, 45
Bateson, Mary Catherine, 39
Behavioural change, 69
Belief modification, 115
Biases
  crafting compelling narratives, 56, 57, 62
  setting the scene, 84–111
  simplifying complex concepts, 136
Biological mechanisms, 41
Blogs, 195
Body language, 177
Bonds, 12, 17, 18, 19, 20, 134, 158, 159, 160, 163
Boomers, 109, 110, 128
Buffett, Warren, 45, 88, 148

C

Case studies, 21, 28, 68, 195, 200, 203, 204, 205, 206, 208
Challenges, 147, 165, 170, 204, 262
  building narrative resilience, 188
  building trust, 184
  case studies, 203
  crafting compelling narratives, 53, 54, 58, 64
  creating relatable character, 65
  creating relatable characters, 66, 67, 69, 70, 71
  economic, 81
  empowering clients, 34
  engaging the audience, 189, 190
  ethics and responsibility, 42, 213, 220, 221, 224
  power of stories, 43, 47, 48
  psychological biases, 109
  setting the scene, 81, 86, 112, 116, 117, 120, 121, 125
  simplifying complex concepts, 150, 153
Challenges creating relatable characters, 69
Characters, 260
  crafting compelling narratives, 57, 61, 62, 63, 64
  creating relatable characters, 65, 68, 70, 71, 75, 76
  power of stories, 49
  proactive and empowered, 70
  relatable, 52, 69, 75
  relatable, 21
  responsibility in storytelling, 213, 226
  setting the scene, 114, 121
Client
  archetypes, 66
  connection, 24
  conversations, 4, 178, 265
  profiles, 53
  relationships, 16, 219, 225, 238, 239, 242, 244, 246, 247, 249, 250, 252, 257, 260, 266
  response, 255
  retention, 16, 219, 247, 263
Cognitive dissonance, 112, 115
Collective responsibility, 44
communication
  impact of storytelling, 241–59
Communication, 194, 198, 231, 235, 237, 238, 239, 240, 259, 264
  channels, 193
  creating relatable characters, 70
  empowering clients, 2, 15, 21, 23, 28, 29, 30, 31
  engaging the audience, 186, 189
  financial, 77
  power of stories, 41, 43, 46, 47
  pre-meeting, 29, 30
  responsibility in storytelling, 210, 211, 221, 222, 224
  setting the scene, 116, 125, 128
  simplifying complex concepts, 129, 164
  styles, 28
Comparative narrative strategies, 114
Compound interest, 40, 42, 55, 64, 131, 133, 164, 194, 195, 197, 210, 216, 218, 236
Compounding, 132
Confidence, 243
Confidentiality, 68, 76, 213
Confirmation bias, 92, 93
Context, 187, 198
  creating relatable characters, 75
  empowering clients, 12, 26, 30
  responsibility in storytelling, 212, 219, 221, 226
  setting the scene, 77, 78, 79, 82, 117, 119, 122, 125, 127, 128
  simplifying complex concepts, 159, 163
Continuous improvement, 236, 240, 252
Conversational transitions, 186
Core message, 51, 52, 54, 55, 58, 62, 64, 228
Credibility, 62, 64, 68, 76, 169, 171, 184, 204, 208, 222

Cultural backgrounds, 81, 111
Cultural conditioning, 78, 109, 112, 113
Cultural expectations, 72

D

Data, 167, 175, 182, 184, 198, 230, 260, 261, 262
    empowering clients, 2, 30
    impact of storytelling, 243
    power of stories, 40, 41, 45, 48, 50
    responsibility in storytelling, 214
    setting the scene, 85
    simplifying complex concepts, 136, 151
    techonology, 148
Debt management, 205, 207
Decision-making, 172, 173, 261
    creating relatable characters, 66, 67, 71
    empowering clients, 3, 37
    impact of storytelling, 241, 243, 258
    power of stories, 41, 42, 45, 50
    psychological biases, 84, 85, 97, 101, 103, 110
    responsibility in storytelling, 220
    setting the scene, 79, 82, 83, 84, 85, 93, 95, 112, 117, 128
    simplifying complex concepts, 136, 162
Deep listening, 174
Demographics, 66, 67
Digital age, 221
Digital platforms, 16, 111
Digital presence, 29
Discomfort, 5, 12, 13, 14, 142, 143, 145, 172, 231
Diversification, 187, 195, 228, 233, 234
    crafting compelling narratives, 52, 55, 59, 64
    creating relatable characters, 69
    power of stories, 47
    responsibility in storytelling, 211, 217
    setting the scene, 121
    simplifying complex concepts, 130, 135, 160, 161, 163

E

Economic hardship, 81
Economic stability, 81, 109
Education costs, 69
Eisenberg, Bryan, 227
Emotional
    appeals, 219
    associations, 112, 113
    connection, 17, 57, 63
    decision-maker, 28, 30
    decision-makers, 37
    engagement, 41, 42, 69
    intelligence, 70, 72, 116, 126, 199, 201
    investing, 171
    reactions, 25
    reassurance, 119
    resonance, 48, 150, 187, 195, 201, 217
    responses, 22, 90, 155, 173
    security, 72
Empathy, 172, 173, 174, 175, 177, 181, 182, 184, 199, 235
    creating relatable characters, 70, 72
    power of stories, 42
    setting the scene, 78, 112, 114, 115, 119, 126, 127
Empathy Mapping Framework, 173
Engagement, 21, 120, 177, 222, 244, 245
Estate planning, 60
Ethical considerations, 21, 207, 217, 224
Ethical dilemmas, 216, 217
Ethical responsibilities, 121
Ethics, 209
Exercises, 227, 232
Experiential learning, 43
Exponential growth, 133

F

Fear, 173, 174, 175, 176, 178, 180, 182, 183, 184, 188, 199, 206, 261, 263
  crafting compelling narratives, 54, 55, 56, 57, 61
  creating relatable characters, 67, 71, 72, 73, 74, 76
  empowering clients, 3, 15, 16, 22
  power of stories, 47
  responsibility in storytelling, 211, 217, 219, 226
  risk, 149
  setting the scene, 79, 80, 122, 125
  simplifying complex concepts, 134, 135, 138, 142, 143, 146, 155, 157, 160, 161
Federer Principle, 190, 192
Federer, Roger, 190
Feedback, 48, 75, 161, 197, 201, 222, 227, 231, 236, 237, 239, 240, 254, 256, 264
Financial
  belief systems, 112
  beliefs, 113, 174
  crisis, 16, 45, 61, 87, 118, 142, 167, 181, 195, 212
  education, 28
  erosion, 124
  forecasters, 45, 46
  goals, 67, 171
  history, 54, 153
  inadequacy, 175
  independence, 67, 87, 111, 216
  objectives, 7
  planning, 12, 14, 35, 38, 44, 66, 72, 73, 81, 83, 109, 110, 126, 128, 149, 191, 207, 219
  storytelling
    interactive, 46
  strategy, 134
  success, 25, 33, 69, 88, 113, 164, 171, 178, 192
  wisdom, 43, 44, 50, 262
Financial advice, 179, 180, 205, 227
  creating relatable characters, 65, 75
  empowering clients, 2, 4, 13, 14, 27
  power of stories, 43
  psychological biases, 110
  setting the scene, 78, 116, 119, 120, 122, 125, 127, 128
  simplifying complex concepts, 149
Financial advisory, 3, 14, 28, 37, 40, 200
Financial concepts, 173, 183, 187, 188, 194, 196, 199, 228, 232, 233, 235, 238, 239, 240, 259, 264, 265
  crafting compelling narratives, 56, 60, 61, 62, 64
  creating relatable characters, 65, 69, 76
  empowering clients, 3, 16, 17, 21, 24, 37, 40
  impact of storytelling, 242, 243, 247, 248, 249, 250, 253, 255
  power of stories, 43, 44, 45, 47, 50
  psychological biases, 111
  responsibility in storytelling, 213, 224
  setting the scene, 77, 79, 115, 121, 122, 126, 127
  simplifying complex concepts, 130, 131, 150, 155, 162, 163
  technology, 148
Financial decisions, 170, 172, 180, 182, 184, 239, 261, 262, 265
  crafting compelling narratives, 57
  creating relatable characters, 76
  emotion-driven, 37
  empowering clients, 13, 15, 22, 38
  impulsive, 71
  power of stories, 41, 43, 48
  psychological biases, 101, 111
  responsibility in storytelling, 219
  setting the scene, 78, 113, 119, 127
  simplifying complex concepts, 143, 163
  technology, 148
financial journey, 4, 19, 26, 32, 47, 63, 70, 71, 72, 73, 76, 82, 118, 126, 148,

149, 162, 171, 178, 184, 191, 204, 210, 266
Financial stories, 175, 188, 196, 199
   crafting compelling narratives, 60, 64
   creating relatable characters, 71, 72, 76
   empowering clients, 7
   power of stories, 47, 50
   psychological biases, 109, 110
   setting the scene, 79, 115, 116, 117, 121, 128
   simplifying complex concepts, 150
Financial storytelling, 185, 187, 188, 190, 191, 192, 194, 198, 200
   crafting compelling narratives, 62
   creating relatable characters, 65, 66, 69, 72, 73, 76
   empowering clients, 2, 3, 14, 15, 32, 33, 37, 38
   power of stories, 44, 48, 50
   psychological biases, 109, 110, 111
   responsibility in storytelling, 219
   setting the scene, 78, 79, 112, 116, 119, 120, 125, 126, 128
   simplifying complex concepts, 147, 150, 162

G

Gaiman, Neil, 65
Galbraith, John Kenneth, 26
Gambler's fallacy, 101
Generation X, 110
Generation Z, 111
Generations, 44, 67, 81, 87, 109, 111, 113, 128, 134, 254, 261
Get Rich Quick, 176
Goals, 171, 172, 173, 178, 180, 181, 182, 206, 232, 259, 267
   crafting compelling narratives, 52, 53, 54, 59, 61, 62
   creating relatable characters, 66, 70, 75
   empowering clients, 12, 25
   financial, 53

   power of stories, 46
   professional, 72
   psychological biases, 110, 111
   responsibility in storytelling, 210, 214
   setting the scene, 80, 87, 88, 112, 127
   simplifying complex concepts, 136
Greed, 16
Growth, 61, 62, 170, 174, 182, 188, 190, 191, 192, 204, 205, 206, 208, 231, 232, 234, 236, 260, 264, 266
   crafting compelling narratives, 62
   creating relatable characters, 67, 68, 71, 74, 76
   empowering clients, 5, 19, 20, 33, 38
   impact of storytelling, 254
   power of stories, 42, 45, 48
   responsibility in storytelling, 214
   setting the scene, 112
   setting the scene, 78, 87
   setting the scene, 116
   simplifying complex concepts, 131, 133, 134, 136, 150, 153, 155

H

Hazlitt, William, 241
Herd behaviour, 97, 128
Hopes, 3, 71, 72, 76, 78, 79, 122, 125, 134, 188, 204, 217, 261
Human experience, 2, 37, 44, 71, 77, 78, 119, 120, 125, 175, 204
Human-centred stories, 28

I

Imagery, 53, 62, 64, 131, 160, 190
Imagination, 120
Immediate experiences, 86
Income, 33, 35, 67, 74, 99, 114, 176, 207, 216, 229
Indicators, 242, 243, 244
Individual Savings Account (ISA), 17

Inflation, 12, 67, 78, 79, 80, 81, 122, 123, 124, 125, 233
Informed decisions, 62, 63, 127
Inherited beliefs, 113
Initial consultation, 31
Inspiration, 72, 121, 126, 204, 207, 234, 240
Integrity, 120, 223
Intellectual barriers, 15
Intention, 2, 97, 194, 207, 209, 210, 217
Intuition, 71, 187, 241, 258
Investment. *Sic passim*
Investors, 125, 158, 168, 191, 261
    crafting compelling narratives, 57, 59
    creating relatable characters, 73
    empowering clients, 20, 24, 27
    power of stories, 45, 46
    psychological biases, 85, 97
    responsibility in storytelling, 215
    setting the scene, 83, 84, 86, 87, 95, 118, 124, 125
    simplifying complex concepts, 135, 136, 137, 138, 139, 140, 142, 145, 146, 147, 153, 155, 158

J

Jargon, 2, 15, 28, 34, 45, 70, 129, 131, 235, 248
Job market, 81

K

Key indicators, 256
Kinder, George, 3, 4
Kinder's Three Questions, 3, 4, 37

L

Learning, 21, 43, 48, 112, 136, 148, 166, 171, 188, 191, 193, 194, 196, 201, 266

Legacy, 3, 25, 67, 81, 127, 207, 257, 261, 262, 264, 266
Liabilities, 3
Life context, 119
Life transitions, 13, 117, 128
Linguistic analysis software, 31
LinkedIn, 29, 221
Liquidity, 134
Listening, 25, 115, 119, 153, 157, 193, 196, 220, 244, 247
Long-term investing, 16, 60, 133, 160, 186, 195, 197, 264
    crafting compelling narratives, 59
Long-term thinking, 44

M

Macaulay, Thomas Babington, 153
Markets, 137, 138, 142, 143, 146, 153, 155, 160, 168, 184, 212, 215, 219, 238, 263
    crafting compelling narratives, 57, 59
    creating relatable characters, 73, 74
    discounts, 137
    downturn, 84, 117, 118, 157, 167, 170, 191, 206
    downturns, 16, 139, 140, 143, 146, 160, 163, 212, 220, 232
    empowering clients, 23, 24, 26, 34
    fluctuation, 79, 82
    madness, 25
    opportunities, 33
    power of stories, 45, 46
    psychological biases, 97
    setting the scene, 84, 86, 87, 88, 95, 117
Marks, Howard, 137, 144
Memory retention, 41
Mental accounting, 99, 101
Metaphors, 24, 39, 44, 121, 122, 123, 124, 125, 131, 132, 162, 190, 233, 249, 253, 262
Milestones, 118
Millennials, 110, 128

Mindful observation, 241
Mirror Technique, 113
Mortality, 5, 6, 13, 38
Motivations, 3, 13, 66, 69, 173

N

Narrative. Sic passim
    arc, 53, 205
    bias, 56
    client-centred, 220
    creation, 126
    deconstruction, 174
    fear-based, 211
    frameworks, 47
    structure, 54
Narrative Transportation Theory, 69
Neuroplasticity, 43
Neuroscience, 41
Newsletters, 193, 195, 197

O

Observation, 245, 252, 256
Obstacles, 48, 186, 190
Opportunity, 25, 148
Overreaction bias, 95

P

Pain points, 52
Pattern recognition, 45
Patterns, 173, 243, 254
Peace of mind, 35, 169, 211, 219
Persona, 66, 75, 228
Personal experiences, 113, 169
Personal history, 71, 78, 183
Personal pension, 17
Personal stories, 58, 63, 64, 116, 148, 171, 197
Personal transformation, 48
Personalisation, 198, 207, 208
Personality, 18, 23, 28, 31, 37, 66, 76
Personas, 63, 65, 66, 67, 68, 75, 76, 228, 240

Perspective, 86, 139, 148, 151
Planning, 178, 184, 198, 205, 207, 231, 232, 261, 262, 264
    crafting compelling narratives, 51, 60
    creating relatable characters, 65, 66, 67
    empowering clients, 7
    impact of storytelling, 243
    power of stories, 46
    psychological biases, 110, 111
    responsibility in storytelling, 211, 215, 218, 219, 222, 223
    setting the scene, 81, 87
    simplifying complex concepts, 130, 134
Podcasts, 193, 196, 197
Positive outcomes, 34, 69
Poverty, 175
Predictions, 23, 25, 26, 27, 45, 46, 84, 136, 155
Presentations, 197
Prevention, 12, 34
Privacy, 213
Professional network, 30
Profiling, 31, 172
Profits, 137, 152, 153, 154, 161
Prospect theory, 90, 128
Psychological profiling, 66
Psychological safety, 6, 68
Psychology, 26, 34, 41, 45, 82, 90, 97, 99, 115, 137, 142
Psychology of Money, The, 26
Purchasing power, 80, 123, 233
Purpose, 3, 5, 6, 12, 14, 30, 35, 51, 55, 99, 110, 122, 203, 210, 224, 228, 234, 237, 238, 259

R

Rational analysis, 22
Rationality, 217
Real-life examples, 65, 68, 69, 75, 76
Recency bias, 84, 85, 86, 128, 141
Referrals, 16, 247, 248, 249, 250, 252, 258, 263

Reflection, 6, 46, 114, 118, 124, 168, 237, 238, 240, 253, 258
Relatable context, 48
Relevance, 81, 116, 210
Resilience, 43, 47, 52, 62, 64, 72, 76, 110, 125, 126, 136, 160, 163, 178, 188, 190, 191, 192, 205, 212
Resistance, 230
Responsibility, 209
Retirement, 166, 171, 175, 176, 177, 178, 184, 198, 205, 206, 228, 229, 231, 232, 233, 260, 262, 264
   crafting compelling narratives, 54, 55, 61
   creating relatable characters, 65, 66, 67, 69, 70
   empowering clients, 12, 25
   impact of storytelling, 243
   planning, 60, 176
   power of stories, 45
   responsibility in storytelling, 211, 213, 214, 218, 222, 223
   setting the scene, 80, 81, 117
   simplifying complex concepts, 130
Returns, 23
Risk, 57, 60, 121, 146, 148, 149, 168, 174, 211, 212
   assessments, 3
   management, 60, 72, 195
   profile, 3, 11
   tolerance, 53, 54, 66, 174, 210, 215, 254

S

Sceptical client, 28, 30, 37, 180
Scepticism, 179
Security, 169, 175, 176, 182, 188, 205, 237, 264
   creating relatable characters, 66
   empowering clients, 3, 12, 19
   psychological biases, 109
   responsibility in storytelling, 212, 219, 223
   setting the scene, 78, 81, 112, 114, 119, 127
   simplifying complex concepts, 134
Simplicity, 129
Snowball Effect, 131
Social media, 191, 193, 194, 195, 197, 201, 221, 222, 245, 264
Solutions, 69
Stability, 21
Stock market, 17, 20, 40, 58, 88, 135, 136, 138, 151, 153, 154, 163
Stocks, 17, 134
Story-driven approach, 16
storytelling
   manipulative
Storytelling. *Sic passim*
   approach, 27, 48, 194, 242, 245, 247, 248, 249, 252, 256, 258
   art of, 63, 160, 239
   authentic, 165, 182, 183, 184
   client-centred, 256
   contextual, 79, 125
   development, 48
   educational, 220
   ethical, 68, 210, 219, 221, 222, 223, 226
   history of, 43
   impact of, 241, 246
   in psychological insight, 83
   interactive, 46, 50, 187, 197
   live, 196
   manipulative, 211
   skills, 63, 224, 225, 231, 239, 241
   techniques, 21, 37, 46, 183, 239, 264
Strategic insight, 48
Strategic thinking, 47
Strategies, 169, 174, 181, 188, 200, 204, 208, 233, 260
   crafting compelling narratives, 51, 53, 54
   creating relatable characters, 67, 69
   empowering clients, 8
   impact of storytelling, 243
   power of stories, 40
   psychological biases, 110

responsibility in storytelling, 212, 215
setting the scene, 80, 95, 112, 113, 114, 120, 124, 127
simplifying complex concepts, 133, 134, 135, 150
Success, 1, 69, 147, 190
Sutherland, Rory, 39

T

Tax strategies, 3, 13
Technical analysis, 26, 117, 130
Technical concepts, 48, 261
Technical expertise, 260
Techniques, 29, 31, 122, 174, 185, 187, 231
Technological innovation, 111
Technology, 24, 25, 31, 47, 111, 121, 135, 148, 177, 199, 211, 215, 256
Technology-assisted profiling, 31
Templeton, Sir John, 85
Timing, 22, 26, 116, 119, 125, 128, 142, 215, 216, 217
Tolerance, 88
Tone of voice, 177
Tools, 83, 172, 195, 199, 231, 237, 260
 communication, 253, 257
 crafting compelling narratives, 60, 64
 creating relatable characters, 72
 empowering clients, 22, 31, 32, 37
 financial, 164
 power of stories, 41, 43, 45, 46, 47
 psychological biases, 111
 setting the scene, 121, 126, 127
 simplifying complex concepts, 131, 147, 162, 163
 technology, 148
Transformative potential, 48
Transparency, 210
Trends, 57, 78, 81, 86, 97, 120, 146, 172, 176, 199, 210
Trust, 165, 167, 178, 179, 180, 182, 184, 193, 207, 234, 235, 239, 259
 crafting compelling narratives, 57, 61, 62, 64
 creating relatable characters, 74
 empowering clients, 1, 2, 21, 23, 37
 power of stories, 41, 42, 45
 responsibility in storytelling, 209, 210, 213, 217, 219, 220, 223
 setting the scene, 125
 simplifying complex concepts, 149
Truthfulness, 210

U

Uncertainty, 166, 168, 171, 179, 182, 198, 199, 204, 205, 206, 265
 crafting compelling narratives, 54
 creating relatable characters, 70, 71, 72, 73, 74, 76
 empowering clients, 22, 23, 24, 26
 power of stories, 47
 psychological biases, 84, 97, 109, 110
 responsibility in storytelling, 210
 setting the scene, 117, 118, 126
 simplifying complex concepts, 153
Unconscious scripts, 113
Unrealistic outcomes, 212

V

Validation, 248
Values, 5, 13, 37, 53, 54, 67, 86, 110, 166, 170, 172, 217, 220, 222
Video, 193, 195, 197
Visual metaphor, 17, 24, 37
Vocal technique, 189
Vulnerability, 68, 71, 76, 166, 167, 174, 205, 220, 235

W

Wall Street, 45
Wealth, 59, 135, 177, 207
 accumulation, 35, 110
 crafting compelling narratives, 54

creating relatable characters, 67
empowering clients, 4, 5, 14, 29, 35
psychological biases, 110, 111
responsibility in storytelling, 210
setting the scene, 80, 87, 88, 113
simplifying complex concepts, 132, 135
Webinars, 193, 197

X

Xunzi, 1

Y

Young investors, 74

Printed in Dunstable, United Kingdom